POLITICAL BEHAVIOR OF THE AMERICAN ELECTORATE

William H. Flanigan
UNIVERSITY OF MINNESOTA

SECOND EDITION

Political Behavior
of the
American Electorate

Allyn and Bacon, Inc., Boston

To My Parents

Fourth printing . . . January, 1973

Acknowledgments

The following analysis and description of the American electorate is heavily dependent on the work of others. Until recently, extensive analysis of the research findings and data collected by another social scientist was limited to an examination of published tables, but there have been significant changes since 1960. The major studies of American public opinion and voting behavior are now available to scholars throughout the world for further analysis and examination.

These developments in political analysis have depended on the cooperation of many individuals, but the efforts of two men associated with the Survey Research Center at the University of Michigan deserve special mention. For a number of years Angus Campbell has opened the archives of the Survey Research Center to outside scholars, and I have drawn on the work of many, most notably V. O. Key, who have benefited from the generosity and assistance of Angus Campbell and the Survey Research Center. Warren Miller has directed the organization and expansion of these activities through the creation of the Inter-university Consortium for Political Research. The Consortium, which is composed of the new Center for Political Studies and about 140 departments of political science, has not only made available the archives of the Survey Research Center to a wide clientele but has also made available other major data collections on the same basis.

This study is completely dependent on Survey Research Center data provided by the Inter-university Consortium for

Political Research, and I am pleased to acknowledge my great debt to the individuals in both organizations who have contributed to the establishment of these resources and services. I must hasten to add that neither the Survey Research Center nor the Consortium bears any responsibility for the analysis and interpretations presented here. Indeed the hazard of their efforts to provide open archives is the sort of reinterpretation and reanalysis which follows, and I can only hope that the weaknesses of this work will not reflect on the general worthiness and excellence of the Consortium and the Survey Research Center.

I must also express my debt to the director of the Social Science Research Facilities Center at the University of Minnesota for his assistance with the data processing and to Gloria Priem for typing the manuscript. Among the many students at Minnesota who helped with the analysis I am particularly indebted to Jim Dyer, Doug Frisbie, Caroline Harlow, John Pierce, and Nancy Zingale for genially and competently handling so many of the laborious details in the preparation of the tables. Again these acknowledgments do not diminish my responsibility for the errors that follow, but they qualify considerably the credit I am due.

W.H.F.

Contents

Introduction

The American electoral system is one of the most fascinating of all political institutions. Not only do American campaigns and elections provide a colorful and entertaining array of political practices, but also the political party system, the candidates' appeal to the public, and the ultimate selection and rejection of political leaders represent a successful and time-tested democratic decision-making mechanism the equal of any in human history. For all that, the American electoral system does not operate perfectly, and in some ways it does not operate well at all. This introductory text is not an evaluation of the American electoral system; rather, it explores the system's behavior during the past couple of decades. Voting behavior and political opinions of the American public, as well as some explanations of these major political patterns, are the central concerns of this volume.

MAJOR VOTING STUDIES

It is easy to categorize the major voting studies of the American electorate according to the scholars and research institutions that conducted the studies. The first important study of voting behavior and political opinion relying on survey research techniques was directed by Paul Lazarsfeld, who was interested in the impact of mass media on individual vote choice during a Presidential campaign. Lazarsfeld selected a single community, Erie County in Ohio, for his study during the 1940 Presidential campaign; the publication of his findings, *The People's Choice,*[1] became a major work of social analysis. In 1948 Lazarsfeld, Bernard Berelson, and William McPhee of the Bureau of Applied Social Research at Columbia University conducted a second political study in Elmira, New York, then published their findings in *Voting.*[2] Several major findings in political research emerged from these two studies: the cross pressure hypothesis, opinion leadership, selective perception. Up to this point the important public opinion studies were of single communities and were conducted entirely by sociologists.

In 1948 the newspaper polls predicted a Republican victory in the Dewey-Truman race for President, while a Survey Research Center national survey showed Truman winning, thereby publicizing the more scientific sampling used in academic polling. This success promoted a national political survey during the 1952 Presidential election, which was reported in *The Voter Decides*[3] and which emphasized partisanship, issues, and candidate images. National political studies have been made by the Survey Research Center every two years since 1952, and the following analysis depends heavily on these studies up to and including the 1968 survey. The most impressive study, *The American Voter,*[4] by Campbell, Converse, Miller, and Stokes, based mainly on the 1952 and 1956 national surveys, continued the emphasis on partisanship and political attitudes. It is required reading for anyone with a serious interest in American political behavior. Most of the following analysis depends heavily on *The American Voter,* both for substantive findings about the electorate and for analytic organization of the material. The most recent publication by these authors, *Elections and the Political Order,*[5] covers subsequent

[1] Paul Lazarsfeld, Bernard Berelson, and Hazel Gaudet, *The People's Choice* (New York: Columbia University Press, 1944).

[2] Bernard R. Berelson, Paul F. Lazarsfeld, and William N. McPhee, *Voting* (Chicago: University of Chicago Press, 1954).

[3] Angus Campbell, Gerald Gurin, and Warren Miller, *The Voter Decides* (Evanston: Row, Peterson and Co., 1954).

[4] Angus Campbell et al., *The American Voter* (New York: John Wiley and Sons, 1960).

[5] Angus Campbell et al., *Elections and the Political Order* (New York: John Wiley and Sons, 1966).

elections and pursues the main themes of *The American Voter* in more complex analysis.

The most extensive survey of research on American political behavior is *Political Life,*[6] by Robert Lane; this should be supplemented by bibliographic essays in *Essays on the Behavioral Study of Politics,*[7] edited by Austin Ranney, or *The Behavioral Persuasion in Politics,*[8] by Heinz Eulau. The best collections of readings on political behavior currently available appear to be *Political Opinion and Electoral Behavior,*[9] by Dreyer and Rosenbaum, and *Politics and Social Life,*[10] by Polsby, Dentler, and Smith. Several recent studies of importance deal with special topics. A highly sophisticated analysis of black political behavior in the South is *Negroes and the New Southern Politics,*[11] by Matthews and Prothro. Pool, Abelson, and Popkin report an unusual and interesting effort at simulating the American electorate in *Candidates, Issues and Strategies;*[12] and *The Electoral Process,*[13] edited by Jennings and Zeigler, is a good collection on campaigns and elections. V. O. Key's last book, *The Responsible Electorate,*[14] discusses the reasoned nature of attitudes and behavior in the American public which was one of the concerns of his earlier book, *Public Opinion and American Democracy.*[15] A general survey of socialization processes appears in Kenneth Langton's *Political Socialization.*[16]

[6] Robert E. Lane, *Political Life* (New York: The Free Press, 1959).

[7] Austin Ranney, *Essays on the Behavioral Study of Politics* (Urbana: University of Illinois Press, 1962).

[8] Heinz Eulau, *The Behavioral Persuasion in Politics* (New York: Random House, 1965).

[9] Edward Dreyer and Walter Rosenbaum, eds., *Political Opinion and Electoral Behavior* (Belmont, Calif.: Wadsworth Publishing Co., 1966).

[10] Nelson W. Polsby, Robert A. Dentler, and Paul A. Smith, *Politics and Social Life: An Introduction to Political Behavior* (Boston: Houghton Mifflin Company, 1963).

[11] Donald Matthews and James Prothro, *Negroes and the New Southern Politics* (New York: Harcourt, Brace and World, 1967).

[12] Ithiel de Sola Pool, Robert Abelson, and Samuel Popkin, *Candidates, Issues and Strategies* (Cambridge, Mass.: The M.I.T. Press, 1964).

[13] M. Kent Jennings and L. Harmon Zeigler, eds., *The Electoral Process* (Englewood Cliffs, N.J.: Prentice-Hall, 1966).

[14] V. O. Key, Jr., *The Responsible Electorate* (Cambridge, Mass.: Belknap Press of Harvard University Press, 1966).

[15] V. O. Key, Jr., *Public Opinion and American Democracy* (New York: Alfred A. Knopf, 1961).

[16] Kenneth P. Langton, *Political Socialization* (New York: Oxford University Press, 1969).

A comparative analysis of political socialization by Almond and Verba, *The Civic Culture*,[17] includes the United States along with four other countries and puts American political behavior in a different perspective, as does Robert Alford's *Party and Society*,[18] a comparative study of voting behavior. Among several theoretical works dealing with public opinion and voting, the most prominent are *An Economic Theory of Democracy*,[19] by Anthony Downs, and *A Preface to Democratic Theory*,[20] by Robert Dahl. *Political Man*,[21] by S. M. Lipset, covers numerous topics in public opinion and voting behavior, including ideology, which is the central concern of *Political Ideology*,[22] by Robert Lane, and *The Political Beliefs of Americans*,[23] by Lloyd Free and Hadley Cantril. The work of Herbert McClosky has dealt with ideology and political psychology but as yet appears only in article form. More recently Robert Lane and Fred Greenstein have focused on the psychology of political behavior.[24] The Inter-university Consortium for Political Research has provided an excellent volume on political indices, *Measures of Political Attitudes*.[25]

Not all of the significant studies of American voting behavior have centered around attitudes. V. O. Key demonstrated the applications of the analysis of election returns for describing and understanding political behavior in *American State Politics*,[26] and recently Milton Cummings has written in the same tradition in

[17]Gabriel Almond and Sidney Verba, *The Civic Culture* (Princeton, N.J.: Princeton University Press, 1963).

[18]Robert R. Alford, *Party and Society* (Chicago: Rand McNally and Company, 1963).

[19]Anthony Downs, *An Economic Theory of Democracy* (New York: Harper and Brothers, 1957).

[20]Robert A. Dahl, *A Preface to Democratic Theory* (Chicago: University of Chicago Press, 1956).

[21]Seymour M. Lipset, *Political Man* (Garden City, N.Y.: Doubleday and Company, 1960).

[22]Robert E. Lane, *Political Ideology* (New York: The Free Press, 1962).

[23]Lloyd A. Free and Hadley Cantril, *The Political Beliefs of Americans* (New York: Simon and Schuster, 1968).

[24]Robert E. Lane, *Political Thinking and Consciousness* (Chicago: Markham Publishing Co., 1969); Fred J. Greenstein, *Personality and Politics* (Chicago: Markham Publishing Co., 1969).

[25]John P. Robinson, Jerrold G. Rusk, and Kendra B. Head, *Measures of Political Attitudes* (Ann Arbor, Mich.: Institute for Social Research, 1968).

[26]V. O. Key, Jr., *American State Politics* (New York: Alfred A. Knopf, 1956).

Congressmen and the Electorate. [27] At present there is a practically complete collection of national election returns for major offices recorded by counties and available through the Inter-university Consortium for Political Research. These data will allow more elaborate historical election analysis than heretofore. European scholars have done more with aggregate data; three excellent collections focusing on European electoral behavior have appeared in recent years: Lipset and Rokkan, *Party Systems and Voter Alignments,*[28] Dahl, *Political Oppositions in Western Democracies,*[29] and Dogan and Rokkan, *Quantitative Ecological Analysis in the Social Sciences.*[30]

By drawing on these studies and data provided through the Inter-university Consortium for Political Research at the University of Michigan, I will summarize the analysis of American political behavior around five major topics. Chapter 1 will explore the characteristics of the electorate during the past hundred years and then concentrate on explanations of non-participation and particularly of non-voting at the present time. In chapter 2 the broad outlines of partisan political forces are described, and the three main categories of American voters—Republicans, Democrats, and independents—are discussed. The next chapter investigates the social background of partisans and independents, and some of the main social explanations of political behavior are described with an emphasis on primary groups, secondary groups, and social class. In chapter 4 an alternative to social and economic explanations of political behavior, political opinions, and ideology is considered, with emphasis on psychological factors. In the final chapter the focus is on political campaigns and on the factors which influence the outcome of elections.

In effect, after the initial consideration of suffrage and turnout, the non-participants in the electoral system are dropped from consideration. The two major factors accounting for complete non-participation in civic activities are legal restrictions and

[27]Milton Cummings, *Congressmen and the Electorate* (New York: The Free Press, 1966).

[28]Seymour M. Lipset and Stein Rokkan, *Party System and Voter Alignments: Cross National Perspectives* (New York: The Free Press, 1967).

[29]Robert A. Dahl, ed., *Political Oppositions in Western Democracies* (New Haven: Yale University Press, 1966).

[30]Mattei Dogan and Stein Rokkan, eds., *Quantitative Ecological Analysis in the Social Sciences* (Cambridge, Mass.: The M.I.T. Press, 1969).

apathy, but these two factors are not useful in accounting for variation in more active forms of political behavior. Partisanship, which is the major determinant of political behavior in the American setting, appears to have far greater impact on vote choice and attitudes than either social class or political ideology. These three elements—partisanship, social class, and ideology—suggest the broad outline of explanation of political behavior: during an individual's life, social class and, more generally, social conditions determine ideology and partisanship, which mutually influence each other and in turn determine vote choices and positions on political issues. Throughout this dominant pattern of relationships, personality characteristics modify or exaggerate the impact of the main forces at work. Because in American society the social conditions are so varied, the political relationships are not simple and dramatic, but rather present a diffuse pattern of complex interrelationships. These patterns are the focus of subsequent chapters.

There is a complication in the examination of political behavior over time. Not only does the electorate shift its policy preference, becoming more or less liberal, more or less internationalist, but the parties shift as well. If both the parties and the electorate shift as they seemingly have in recent decades, there may be a deceptive stability in voting patterns that conceals a large shift in policy implications. The following analysis ignores political leaders and party platforms while concentrating on the public. The public should be viewed as the background against which Presidents, legislators, and political leaders generally seek public office and make policy. The public not only represents a potential influence on many aspects of the policy-making process, but is, as well, a persistently interesting political phenomenon quite apart from its immediate implications for the operation of American government.

1

Suffrage and Turnout

In the United States today over 60 percent of all adults vote in Presidential elections, and all but a rather small minority of adults are eligible to register to vote if they choose to do so. Widespread participation of all adults in elections and the nearly universal extension of suffrage are fairly recent developments in our political history. During most of the 180 years of American electoral history, a minority of adults have been eligible to vote.

Through the amendments to the United States Constitution, there have been two major extensions of suffrage; in practice and in law development has been more uneven.[1] These extensions of suffrage have not been easy or inevitable; I suggest two factors which account for extensions of suffrage or explain the existence of political forces which bring them about: *In stable political systems the extension of suffrage will result from (1) a widely shared commitment to moral principles which entail further grants of suffrage, and (2) the expectation among political leaders that the newly enfranchised will support their policy preferences.*

The political rhetoric of America carries strong themes of egalitarian democracy, and, normally, young people who go through the political and civic training in the educational system absorb the ideals of individualism and equality. American national-

---

[1] For a discussion of the legal history of civil rights, most American government textbooks will provide a general introduction.

ism, with the myths of the frontier and the melting pot, has justified these values. In part, the goals of American education are
participation in, and support of, American democracy. Although
seldom explicitly political in their indoctrination, American
religious institutions have reinforced these themes in the political
culture. American literature and theater contribute to political
education in these values. The result is that most Americans have
had a commitment to equality, individualism, and democracy,
which has provided a basis for support of extensions of voting
rights.

To be sure, there have been counterthemes in American
political culture. As in any complex society, there are conflicting
ideals and perspectives which contradict and undermine one
another. It is merely a contention—which will not be proved—that
American political culture has been dominated by ideas and beliefs
which favored the extension of voting rights and that when suffrage has been restricted it has been treated as an exception to
more general political principles. Usually it requires a tremendous
effort for a subculture to maintain beliefs and values in conflict
with the main culture. The Southern way of life can be viewed as
subculture values and social practices aimed in part at keeping the
black from being covered by the general beliefs in equality and
individual rights. Although successful, the imposition of the
Southern subculture has entailed great social and psychological
costs.

In the two dramatic extensions of suffrage, to blacks and to
women, there have been obvious expectations on the part of
political leaders as to what policies the newly enfranchised would
support. The black voters in the South after the Civil War were
one of the mechanisms of anticipated Republican domination of
Southern states, and perhaps most Southern states passed through
a period where there was at least some chance of combining the
votes of blacks and Populists into a governing majority. The
intense prejudice of the whites and the difficulty in maintaining
the enfranchisement of the black kept this strategy an un-
promising one under most circumstances, but a significant element
in the Republican enthusiasm for black suffrage was the knowl-
edge that Republican votes were being added to the rolls.

There was considerable idealism behind the efforts to enfran-
chise blacks, and the same idealism appears to have supported
suffrage for women. Women were expected to clean up politics

once they had the vote; they were seen optimistically as the cure for corruption in government, as unwavering opponents of alcohol, and as champions of virtue in the electorate. Reformers of all sorts hopefully encouraged the enfranchisement of women as a means of promoting their own goals.

Another aspect of the extension of suffrage in the United States is more uncommon in stable democratic regimes. The addition of states in the frontier expansion across the continent added millions of voters to the electorate throughout the nineteenth century. This vast geographical expansion of the nation kept the electorate overwhelmingly rural. During the decades immediately prior to the Civil War, the politics of slavery dominated the political decisions on additions of states, with accompanying expectations as to the policy impact of expansion. To some degree, the extensions of state boundaries amounted to following the nation's electorate westward.

EXTENSIONS OF SUFFRAGE

In the colonial period and the early years of the Republic, suffrage was commonly restricted to white males with varying amounts of property; thus, only a small proportion of the adult population was eligible to vote. The severity of the impact of the property requirements varied from state to state; their enforcement varied perhaps even more. Gradually the amount of property held or the amount of taxes paid to obtain suffrage was reduced. Sometimes these changes were hard-won reforms enacted by state legislatures or by state constitutional changes, but in other circumstances practical considerations led to substantial reforms. For example, in the Western frontier areas in the nineteenth century, delays in acquiring final title to land holdings made it inexpedient to impose property requirements. Very early in American history in some local elections, candidates would agree among themselves that all white males could vote rather than try to impose complicated restrictions on the electorate. Only in more settled communities can refined restrictions of suffrage be effectively imposed. In sections of the East, powerful landlords controlled the votes of tenants and supported their enfranchisement.[2]

[2] Chilton Williamson, *American Suffrage from Property to Democracy 1760-1860* (Princeton: Princeton University Press, 1960), especially pp. 138-81.

After granting suffrage to white males, the next major change was the enfranchisement of blacks and subsequently their disfranchisement in the South. (This aspect of American electoral patterns is discussed below.) The next major extension of voting rights was suffrage for women. As Figure 1.1 illustrates for the extension of suffrage in the United States, the enfranchisement of women was the most dramatic increase in eligible voters. During the years after World War II, only a very small proportion of all adults were not eligible to vote. Throughout American history there have been different state and local election practices, which means that there is no single set of suffrage requirements that can be used as a basis for deciding exactly who belongs to the electorate at any one time. In fact, there were many different electorates with different characteristics. The most recent extension of suffrage was the lowering of the voting age to eighteen.

FIGURE 1.1
The Proportion of the Adult Population Eligible to Register to Vote, 1860-1970

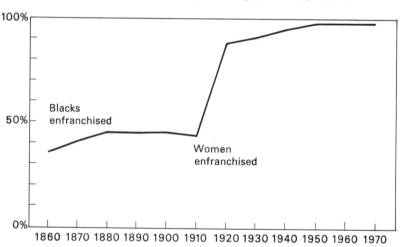

Sources: Robert Lane, *Political Life* (New York: The Free Press of Glencoe, 1959), p. 21; U.S. Bureau of the Census, *Statistical Abstract of the United States: 1969* (90th edition), Washington, D.C., 1969, p. 369.

Although we do not have extensive data on the characteristics of the national electorate during the first century of the Republic, some reasonable inferences can be made from the suffrage laws and descriptive data.[3] Of course, during the early years of the Republic, almost all voters resided in rural areas, whereas the electorate has become steadily more urban over 150 years. By the mid-twentieth century the electorate had become predominantly city and town dwellers. The literacy rate of the electorate was high from the beginning, although the level of education was not. During the nineteenth century, only a very small fraction of Americans graduated from high school. About 2 or 3 percent of the seventeen-year-olds in a given year graduated from high school in 1870 and 1880, but the rate increased rapidly during the first half of the twentieth century to the point where now about two-thirds of the seventeen-year-olds graduate from high school. When blacks were enfranchised after the Civil War, only about half of them had recently been slaves, but the overwhelming majority were illiterate. The illiteracy rate among blacks has steadily declined and at the present approaches the very low rate among whites. (The somewhat higher rate among blacks is mainly the result of illiteracy among older blacks in the population.) Naturalized citizens—never a large proportion of the electorate—are a decreasing feature of the electorate. Additional data would probably show that the peak of naturalized citizens in the electorate never exceeded 25 percent. For all the unpleasant aspects of the reception and treatment of immigrants, the political system accommodated millions of people from abroad without great stress.

To summarize these data, the voters of 1789 can be described as white male adults who held some property. In the most permissive states, 80 percent or more of the white male adults may have been eligible to vote; in the most restrictive states, less than 10 percent were eligible to vote. By 1850 property qualifications still existed in some states, but in many areas restrictions on white males had all but disappeared. After the Civil War, blacks were added to the electorate and held the franchise for about thirty years, when most blacks were disfranchised in state after state. By the early part of the twentieth century, some blacks enjoyed the vote in certain areas, and women had acquired the vote in a variety of types of elections, but the bulk of the electorate were white

---

[3] U.S. Bureau of the Census, *Historical Statistics of the United States, Colonial Times to 1957; Continuation to 1962 and Revisions* (U.S. Government Printing Office, Washington, D.C., 1965), p. 207, p. 65, p. 9.

males. During this period, large numbers of immigrants joined the electorate. After 1920 more and more women joined the electorate, and by 1950 in the North the electorate and the adult population were roughly equivalent. In 1950 in the South, large numbers of women and blacks were still outside the electorate, but this has changed steadily in recent years.

TURNOUT AND INTEREST

One of two general explanations for participation in elections is that *high turnout is a result of intense competition and strong party organizations*. These two factors are interrelated insofar as competition becomes more intense, with strong party organizations making greater and greater efforts to bring in the marginally involved citizens. The other explanation is that *high turnout is a result of greater interest in the electorate; low turnout a result of little interest*. Both explanations have some validity, but the second is much better supported by evidence than the first. In recent elections, competition and party organization have had much less impact on turnout than the level of interest in the electorate. The expected relationship of interest, involvement, and information with the turnout in elections is shown in Figure 1.2; this relationship is confirmed by recent data based on survey research in many countries. Presidential elections are high interest and high turnout elections, off-year Congressional elections are moderate interest and moderate turnout elections, and ordinary primary elections are low interest and low turnout elections.

Deserving of notice are two "deviant" cases, contrary to the expected relationship between turnout and interest. The first deviant case, labeled "alienation," of high interest and little or no turnout may be a situation of voluntary alienation in which individuals withdraw from political participation purposefully. Their high level of interest and information implies that they withdraw for some reason; they are dissatisfied with, or offended by, the political system. "Nonvoluntary alienation" refers to situations in which interested potential voters are prevented from participating. Both situations are dangerous to the political system in that highly interested and informed citizens who refuse to participate have the potential for extremely disruptive activities.

FIGURE 1.2

Hypothetical Relationships between Electoral Turnout and Levels of Interest, Involvement, and Information

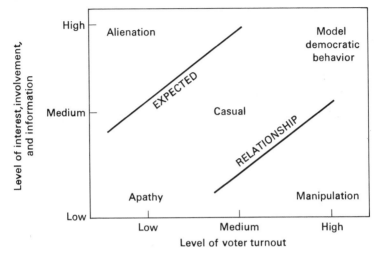

So far as we know, alienation in this form is very uncommon in American politics. In the fall of 1968 there was speculation that large numbers of potential voters were dissatisfied with the candidates and would not cast a ballot for President. While the election of 1968 had a lower turnout than 1964, there is no reason to believe that a sizable proportion of the non-voters were positively alienated.[4]

The second deviant case, low interest and high turnout, labeled "manipulation," refers to a situation in which individuals with little information or interest become involved in voting. Presumably this "manipulation" is achieved by getting individuals to vote either through coercion or by highly stimulating and arousing appeals. Coercive methods for assuring turnout may range from police-state orders to fines for failure to vote. More common in the American political system are exceptionally moving or alarming appeals, bringing to the polls people who are so unsophisticated that they are easily moved. As it is possible to inspire very high levels of turnout by emotional, inflammatory appeals, this is

[4] Philip E. Converse, Warren E. Miller, Jerrold D. Rusk, and Arthur C. Wolfe, "Continuity and Change in American Politics: Parties and Issues in the 1968 Election," *American Political Science Review,* Vol. 63 (December, 1969), 1093-4.

perhaps what happened for many years in the United States after the Civil War. We know that campaigns were marked by extreme appeals, and we know that there were very high levels of turnout. We cannot be sure about interest, involvement, and information; but, since education levels were low, we might reasonably suspect that there were lower levels of interest and information than during the twentieth century. We will return to a discussion of this situation below.

We expect the relationship between turnout and interest to account for the lower levels of turnout in Congressional elections or in primary elections as a reflection of lower interest in those elections. More specifically, *we not only expect different levels of interest from one type of election to another but we also expect differences in the level of turnout for any given type of election to vary with the amount of interest in that particular race.*

A number of elements would seem to influence the amount of interest in an election. The differences in levels of interest from Presidential elections to Congressional elections to party elections can be viewed as a result of:

1)   differences in media coverage given the election;
2)   significance attached by voters to the office;
3)   importance of issues raised in the campaign;
4)   attractiveness of candidates.

Variation in these factors leads to what Angus Campbell has called "high stimulus" and "low stimulus" elections.[5]

Newspapers and television give far more coverage to the activities and speeches of Presidential candidates than to Congressional candidates. Even the most indifferent citizen comes to possess impressions and some information about Presidential candidates and their campaign. This bombardment through the mass media awakens the relatively uninterested and often provides them with some reason for bothering to vote. This is not nearly so likely to happen in other election campaigns, where only the motivated citizens will become informed and concerned to any degree. Even so, a week or so after the election, a substantial proportion of the voters will not recall the name of the Congressional candidate for whom they voted.

---

[5] Angus Campbell et al., *Elections and the Political Order* (New York: John Wiley and Sons, 1966), pp. 40-62.

The outcome of elections in the United States is not viewed as desperately serious by most voters. There is an easygoing attitude toward most contests and a feeling that it does not matter greatly who wins. Few elections take on great significance for many voters, but there are exceptions. In 1960, for instance, throughout the country some Protestants became concerned over the threat of a Catholic in the White House; for some voters concern over the outcome became intense. Sometimes issues are raised which stimulate interest and concern in the electorate. In 1964 some voters apparently responded with concern to the "trigger-happy" image of Goldwater, but it is difficult to point to dramatic instances of large numbers of voters being much concerned with a particular issue. Most commentators rated 1968 as an exceptionally intense election—and in some ways it surely was—but the electorate generally responded with neither exceptional interest nor concern. There was the lowest level of concern over which party won the presidency of any election since 1952.

Voters may respond to attractive qualities in the candidates. The Eisenhower elections of 1952 and 1956 seem to have offered a candidate attractive enough to motivate otherwise indifferent people to vote, and the same thing happens occasionally in local elections. Still these four factors—media coverage, importance of the office, issue salience, and attractive candidates—are more likely to be present to a high degree in a Presidential election than in lesser races, even though exceptional local races may be strong on all four. This general tendency means that Presidential elections are much more likely to be "high stimulus" elections with high turnout and other elections are likely to be "low stimulus" elections with lighter voting.

TURNOUT IN AMERICAN ELECTIONS

Surely one of the most persistent complaints about the American electoral system is its failure in the twentieth century to achieve the high rates of voter turnout found in other countries and common in this country in the nineteenth century. While democracies around the world frequently record turnout rates over 90 percent, turnout in the United States exceeds 60 percent only in Presidential elections. The unfavorable comparisons are misleading on several grounds, since turnout is computed in different ways in each country. In most foreign countries, rates of turnout are based on lists of registered voters rather than on the total eligible electorate or on the adult population. There are no detailed comparative studies of voting, but the reported rates exaggerate turnout perhaps by 15 percent or more. The rates of turnout in the United States, on the other hand, usually fail to take into account the substantial limitations on eligibility associated with residence requirements and other restrictions. The most careful estimate of American turnout takes into account all the various restrictions and concludes that turnout in the 1960 Presidential election was over 80 percent of the eligible electorate.[6] This rate is about 20 percent higher than the "official" rate in Figure 1.3, but for the convenience of comparison with other years I will use the lower rates in the following discussion.

While suffrage was extended during the past hundred years, there was a decline in the proportion of eligible voters turning out for elections, as shown in Figure 1.3. With each extension of suffrage—and most dramatically the enfranchisement of women in 1920—there is a substantial drop in the proportion voting. During the nineteenth century national turnout appears extremely high—always over 70 percent. The decline in national turnout in Figure 1.3 from shortly before 1900 to 1916 is associated with the restriction of black voting in the South, but this factor does not explain the decline in turnout found elsewhere. This decline in voting also results from the increasing one-party domination of the South as well as elsewhere, since the absence of party competition there resulted in far lower turnout than can be accounted for by the disfranchisement of blacks.

The effective disfranchisement of blacks (and many low-income whites) was accomplished at different times in the states of the old Confederacy, but generally the severe limitations of the electorate did not occur until late in the nineteenth century or shortly after the turn of the twentieth century. Several techniques for disfranchising blacks have been used during the past century in the South, and from time to time some of these techniques have been applied in the North on a more limited basis to restrict the electoral participation of immigrants. The most common methods

[6] William G. Andrews, "American Voting Participation," *The Western Political Quarterly*, Vol. 19 (1966), 639.

FIGURE 1.3

Estimated Turnout of Eligible Voters in Presidential Elections in the South and Non-South, 1860-1968

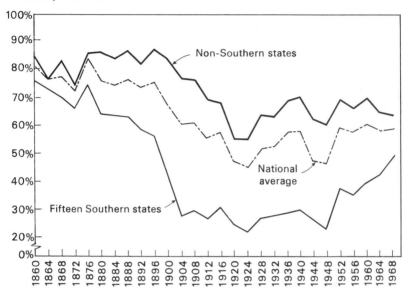

Sources: Robert Lane, *Political Life* (New York: The Free Press of Glencoe, 1959), p. 20; U.S. Bureau of the Census, *Statistical Abstract of the United States: 1969* (90th edition), Washington, D.C., 1969, p. 370; Walter Dean Burnham, "The Changing Shape of the American Political Universe," *American Political Science Review,* Vol. 59 (March, 1965), 11, Figure 1.

have been the poll tax, literacy tests, white primaries, discriminatory administrative procedures, and intimidation. It would be extremely difficult to state precisely what impact these techniques have had at various times, but a few general observations can be made. The blacks' low social and economic circumstances surely contribute to non-participation, since these conditions lead to low interest and non-participation elsewhere and among all groups. Furthermore, in many parts of the South blacks have been offered only anti-black candidates to support—a condition not likely to inspire voter participation.

A study of black registration in 1958 by Matthews and Prothro[7] indicated that Southern states using poll taxes and

---

[7] Donald R. Matthews and James W. Prothro, "Political Factors and Negro Voter Registration in the South," *American Political Science Review,* Vol. 57 (June, 1963), 355-67.

literacy tests inhibited black voter registration. The now-illegal poll tax, a flat fee charged each individual as a prerequisite for registration to vote, was used for years and no doubt disfranchised both poor blacks and poor whites. In recent years it has become less effective, as well as unpopular, with the white voters who have had to pay it while the black, disfranchised by other means, has not paid it. The literacy test has given local officials a device which could be administered in a selective way to permit registration of whites and practically prohibit the registration of blacks. The "standards of literacy" applied in some cases to blacks have precluded registration. Similar administrative devices have blocked the attempts of blacks to register. To remain effective over long periods of time, these devices probably have depended on the threat or use of violence against blacks.

Matthews and Prothro also demonstrate that competitive factions within the Democratic Party are associated with increased black registration, while competition between Republicans and Democrats is not. In addition, the existence of black political and civil rights organizations in a county are associated with increased registration. Surprisingly, in the 1950s incidents of racial violence do not appear to be associated with black registration; that is, high levels of violence do not substantially reduce registration. This does not mean that intimidation is ineffective or that violence serves no purpose, but there is no simple relationship between violence and registration.

The Northern states in Figure 1.3 present a more difficult problem in explanation, since there was a substantial decline in turnout in the first two decades of the twentieth century, and turnout has not returned to its previous levels. The disfranchisement of blacks and whites found in the South cannot account for Northern non-voting. There are two quite different explanations of the decline in voting in the North commencing in the late 1890s.

A persuasive case has been made by Schattschneider[8] and Burnham[9] in their studies of this period. Basically, they contend that there was a high level of party loyalty and political involvement during the late nineteenth century, causing high turnout and

[8] E. E. Schattschneider, *The Semisovereign People* (New York: Holt, Rinehart and Winston, 1960), esp. chap. 5.

[9] Walter Dean Burnham, "The Changing Shape of the American Political Universe," *American Political Science Review*, Vol. 59 (March, 1965), 7-28.

great partisan stability. At some time during the 1890s electoral patterns shifted in such a way that the South became safely Democratic, and most of the rest of the nation came under the domination of the Republican Party. Schattschneider's analysis emphasizes the degree to which this alignment enabled conservatives in both regions to dominate American politics for many years. A consequence of declining competition and greater conservatism throughout the electoral system, according to this line of argument, is a loss of interest in politics accompanied by lower turnout and less partisan loyalty. Burnham emphasizes the disintegration of party voting with more ticket splitting and lower turnout in off-year elections.

Some elements of this account are undeniable. There was a shift in electoral patterns after 1896 with much of the nation changing from competitive to one-party areas. Throughout areas previously characterized by high turnout, straight ticket voting, and stable voting patterns, there were greater fluctuations in turnout and partisan stability.

An alternative set of arguments is consistent with these patterns but gives them a different interpretation. The high rate of turnout may not have been a result of political involvement by an interested, well-informed electorate, but on the contrary may have been possible at all only because of low levels of information and interest. A largely uninformed electorate was aroused to vote by means of extreme and emotional political appeals. Presumably these alarming bits of information in the absence of a more general awareness of what was at stake produced firm commitments to vote. But, by and large, the parties manipulated the electorate—a manipulation possible because the electorate was not well informed.

Furthermore, the party organization "delivered" or "voted" substantial numbers of voters during this period. The remarkable stability of party voting during this period may be a testimony to the corruption of the party organizations. The decline of stable party voting in the early twentieth century coincides with various attacks on political corruption and party machines. In fact, the apparent hostility in the electorate to the parties throughout this period seems inconsistent with extremely high levels of party loyalty. A recent study by Jerrold Rusk[10] shows dramatic changes

[10]Jerrold D. Rusk, "The Effect of the Australian Ballot Reform on Split Ticket Voting: 1876-1908" (Ph.D. diss., University of Michigan, 1968).

in voting patterns associated with electoral reform laws and especially the introduction of the Australian ballot. Prior to the introduction of these reforms, voting was often not secret; ballots prepared by the political parties and limited to one party were distributed to voters, marked, and placed in the ballot box.

The decline in turnout outside the South in subsequent elections may have resulted from the failure of the Democratic Party to offer a sufficiently attractive alternative to draw votes away from the Republicans, who had the advantage of being associated with prosperity and a military victory. Republican dominance was not broken until another depression, except for elections of 1912 and 1916 when the Republicans were divided. The early decades of the twentieth century brought the decline of party machines and increased honesty in electoral activities, both of which could have reduced turnout.

Turnout in national elections, as shown in Figure 1.4, has generally increased in the past forty-five years with the exception of the World War II years and immediately thereafter. There are great differences in turnout among the states concealed within these national data. As Figure 1.3 shows, there are consistently low rates of voting in the South; turnout in Northern states runs around ten percentage points above the national average. The most consistent pattern in Figure 1.4 reveals that in non-Presidential election years there is always a decline in turnout. Even in a Presidential year fewer people vote in Congressional elections, but the dramatic decline in turnout is the 10 to 20 percent decline in voting in the off-year elections. It is reasonable to expect the differences in turnout between North and South to disappear gradually as competition increases, but the different rates of voting in Presidential and Congressional elections are more likely to endure.

Since we have postulated that turnout is in part a function of competition, we might expect the more competitive primary elections in Southern states to have a higher rate of participation than general elections dominated by the Democrats. To some extent this does indeed appear to be the case, but the level of turnout is still about half the higher rates of voting in the North. Apparently the competition in Southern primaries has not had sufficient impact on the political mood of the South to alter basic attitudes toward participation in elections. By 1968, with three-way races between Nixon, Humphrey, and Wallace, in most Southern states

FIGURE 1.4
Turnout of Eligible Voters in Presidential and Congressional Elections, 1920-1968

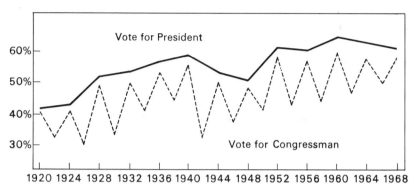

Source: U.S. Bureau of the Census, *Statistical Abstract of the United States: 1969* (90th edition), Washington, D.C., 1969, p. 370.

turnout began to approach the national average as shown in Figure 1.3.

There are other variables related to turnout, as Figure 1.5 shows. Both age and level of education are related to turnout, but

FIGURE 1.5
Turnout in the 1964 Presidential Election according to Age and Education

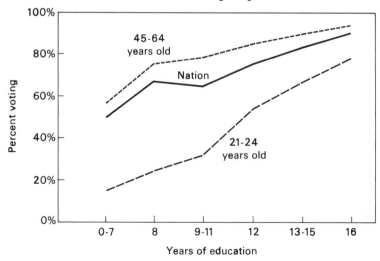

Source: U.S. Bureau of the Census, *Current Population Reports,* Series P-20, No. 143, "Voter Participation in the National Election: November 1964," U.S. Government Printing Office, Washington, D.C., 1965, p. 16.

we know that these variables are also related to interest in politics. For example, both young people and old people are less interested in politics and campaigns than are middle-aged people. College-educated individuals have a higher level of interest; grade school-educated a lower level of interest. Men are more interested in politics than are women. Individuals with higher incomes show more interest than do lower-income individuals. These relationships between turnout and characteristics like age, education, income, and region appear to hold for all elections in much the same way. The more important observation, however, is that the distribution of these personal characteristics for non-voters and voters are about the same in all elections. This means that about the same proportion of non-voters are over sixty-five or have a college education in a Presidential election or in an off-year election. *The social composition of voters and non-voters does not change significantly from one election to the next.*

HABITUAL NON-VOTERS

Over the years, most Americans vote at least occasionally. The fluctuations in turnout bring different individuals to the polls at each election. A rather small proportion of the potential national electorate never votes, about 15 percent in recent years. These habitual non-voters are distinctly unlike those citizens who vote, but most of the non-voters in any particular election are individuals who have voted at least occasionally in the past. We will now turn our attention to these habitual non-participants.

Almost half of the habitual non-voters live in the South. Over two-thirds of these non-participants are women; one-fourth are black. They are disproportionately poor; 22 percent lived in households with incomes under $2,000 in 1964 and the next 35 percent with incomes between $3,000 and $5,000—about twice the rate of low incomes as the rest of the population. About half are young—under thirty—so they have passed up only a few opportunities to vote. One-third have a grade school education or less, and over 60 percent live in working-class households. This group as a whole has very little interest in politics; over 50 percent expressed no interest at all in the Presidential campaign. As a group they are unlikely to have opinions on matters of public policy.

Outside the South in the last fifteen years this group of non-voters has remained constant in size, around 7 or 8 percent of the electorate. Individuals are constantly leaving this category by voting in an election, for by age forty virtually everyone outside the South eligible to vote has voted at least occasionally. The non-voters in the North come from two main sources: young people entering the electorate who do not vote initially, and disfranchised blacks from the South who do not vote immediately in the North because of residence requirements or for some other reason.

NON-VOTING IN THE SOUTH

In the South there has been a steady decrease of permanent non-voters from 38 percent in 1952 to 26 percent four years later, to 18 percent in 1960, and to about 15 percent in 1964 and 1968. This decline in non-voting occurred among both whites and blacks, but it has had a more dramatic impact in reducing permanent non-voters among blacks, as shown in Table 1.1.

TABLE 1.1
The Distribution of Adults Who Have Never Voted according to Race and Sex for the South and Non-South in 1952, 1956, 1960, 1964, and 1968

	1952		1956		1960		1964		1968	
	White	Black	White	Black	White	Black	White	Black	White	Black
SOUTH[a]										
Men	12%	65%	14%	60%	8%	33%	5%	26%	9%	25%
Women	33%	87%	27%	70%	17%	63%	14%	39%	26%	31%
NON-SOUTH[b]										
Men	6%	17%	6%	17%	6%	11%	7%	10%	9%	0%[c]
Women	7%	11%	10%	32%	7%	28%	7%	18%	7%	17%

Source: Survey Research Center, University of Michigan.
[a]The states included in the "South" are Alabama, Arkansas, Florida, Georgia, Kentucky, Louisiana, Maryland, Mississippi, North Carolina, Oklahoma, South Carolina, Tennessee, Texas, Virginia, West Virginia.
[b]The states included in the "Non-South" are the remainder.
[c]This "unrealistic" finding may reflect sampling problems in central cities of the North.

Substantial proportions of blacks still have never voted in the South, but the change from 1952 to 1968 is impressive, and a large proportion of Southern women, both white and black, had never voted in a Presidential election as recently as 1952. In the South there is a persistent tendency for non-voting to be higher among women regardless of race, just as non-voting is higher among blacks regardless of sex. It is not possible from these data to infer how many of these Southern blacks would have participated in a political culture that was more receptive to their activity. It is obvious that Southern blacks, say in 1952, were not engaged in politics up to their potential, since their rate of participation increased in the following years far more rapidly than any change in the level of education and income among blacks.[11]

In 1968 the biggest increase in turnout among these groups was recorded by Southern blacks, who voted at 51 percent—an increase of 7 percent over 1964—while turnout declined in most groups in 1968.[12] During recent years there has been a dramatic change in the political involvement of Southern blacks as shown in Figure 1.6. In 1952, when most Southern blacks had never voted and before the major symbolic events like Little Rock or the demonstrations, the Southern whites had a higher level of interest in politics than blacks, even allowing for educational differences. For the next twelve years, there was an awakening of interest and concern among blacks, resulting by 1964 in a higher level of interest than among whites at each level of education.

To some extent, non-voting Southern blacks are a special case, representing the only sizable bloc of potential voters in the American electorate who are prevented from participating. But a more general explanation of habitual non-voting also applied to this group for many years: *deprived social conditions or inhibiting cultural values lead to low interest in, little concern with, and little information on, politics and that in turn leads to non-voting.*

[11]For the most sophisticated analysis of the political behavior of Southern blacks, see the recent study by Matthews and Prothro, *Negroes and the New Southern Politics,* op. cit. Also see D. R. Matthews and J. W. Prothro, "Southern Racial Attitudes: Conflict, Awareness and Political Change," *The Annals of the American Academy of Political and Social Science,* 344 (November, 1962), 108-21, and "The Concept of Party Image and Its Importance for the Southern Electorate," in M. K. Jennings and L. H. Zeigler, eds., *The Electoral Process* (Englewood Cliffs, N.J.: Prentice-Hall, 1966), pp. 139-74.

[12]U.S. Bureau of the Census, *Current Population Reports,* "Voter Participation in November 1968," Series P-20, No. 177 (December 27, 1968).

FIGURE 1.6
Interest among Southern Whites and Blacks according to Education, 1952, 1964

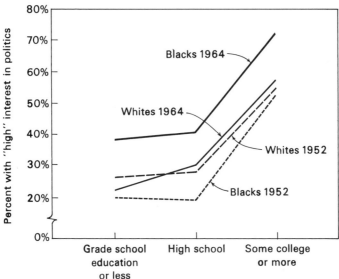

Source: Survey Research Center, University of Michigan.

YOUTHFUL NON-VOTERS

Another group of non-voters forming about 8 percent of the electorate is the young people who pass up their first opportunities to vote. Figure 1.5 shows the tendency of young people not to vote in the first election for which they are eligible regardless of their level of education. Young people are somewhat less interested in politics than are older citizens, but among non-voters young people are more interested in, and concerned with, politics than are older non-voters, as we might expect from their higher level of education. Prior to 1971 only a few states had experimented with extending suffrage to voters below the age of twenty-one. In 1968 this age group, where eligible, turned out to vote at only 36 percent of their full numerical strength.[13]

[13]U.S. Bureau of the Census, *Statistical Abstract of the United States, 1969* (90th edition), Washington, D.C., 1969.

Although there is considerable popular attention given to youthful rebellion, most young people and most older Americans, for that matter, follow the political voting patterns of their parents. Most young people learn to identify with a political party a number of years before they are old enough to vote, and most commonly they follow the party of their parents. Among these new members of the electorate, only 7 percent report that they have switched away from the party of their fathers to the other party; 68 percent are identified with the same party and 24 percent have switched to or continued an independent status. These findings support the generalizations originally documented for a single community by Maccoby, Matthews, and Morton.[14]

Among young people, women are as likely to vote as men, although this characteristic may result from the unsettled circumstances of many young men. Military service, new jobs, the last years of college all contribute to postponing the establishment of residence and the initiation of political participation.

Democrats far outnumber Republicans among new voters, since for thirty years new voters have identified with Democrats by two to one or more. Children of Democratic parents are more likely to remain Democratic than children of Republican parents are likely to remain Republican. Even though 1964 is the most extremely Democratic year among new voters of any election since 1936, the following distributions are only slightly more Democratic than those during the 1950s. In 1964 53 percent identified with the Democratic Party in contrast with 16 percent identified with the Republican Party. Almost one-third consider themselves independents. This means that in terms of the total electorate there has been a net gain of 2 percent to the Democrats about every four years caused by young people entering the electorate with pro-Democratic sympathies. In the last few years new voters have shown less inclination to align themselves with the Democratic Party and have increasingly identified themselves as independents. If unchanged, such erosion of Democratic strength will gradually alter the composition of the electorate.

[14]See E. E. Maccoby, R. E. Matthews, and A. S. Morton, "Youth and Political Change," *Public Opinion Quarterly*, Vol. 18 (1954), 23-29. For more extensive analysis see Kenneth P. Langton, *Political Socialization* (New York: Oxford University Press, 1969), chap. 3.

Although several exceptions have appeared, the basic proposition remains that in the American electorate high turnout is associated with high interest, involvement, and information. The disfranchisement of Southern blacks is the clearest case of coerced non-participation in American electoral history. Young people may offer an example of fairly interested potential voters who are frequently prevented from voting by residential mobility and inconvenience. But for most Americans electoral turnout in all types of elections is related to interest and concern.

2

Partisans and Independents

Generally of greater interest than turnout are partisan voting patterns and the division of votes between Democrats and Republicans. Preferences for candidates vary greatly over the years and within elections between Democrats and Republicans. In some constituencies the variation of support in a single election will create "landslides" for candidates of both parties caused by substantial numbers of voters "splitting their tickets," that is, voting for candidates from more than one party in a single election. In Presidential elections over a third of all voters split their ticket for at least one race. *While under the right circumstances American voters have demonstrated the capacity for highly selective and differentiated support for the candidates offered them by the political parties, under most circumstances the majority of voters cast their votes for the candidates of a single party.*

VARIATION

The variation in partisan preference is even greater over the years, with most voters occasionally deviating from their customary choices. If we consider only a single race like the Presidential contest over time, we find that more than a third of the electorate has voted for Presidential candidates from different parties. In recent years the aggregate vote totals for national elections, shown

in Figure 2.1, reveal a wide range of Democratic fortunes from a
low of 42 percent for Stevenson in his second try against Eisenhower to a high of 61 percent for Johnson against Goldwater in
1964. In 1968 over 13 percent of the voters abandoned the tradi-

FIGURE 2.1
Democratic Presidential and Congressional Votes, 1928-1968

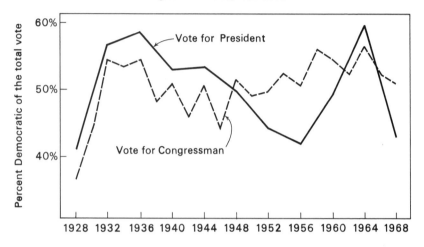

Sources: U.S. Bureau of the Census, *Statistical Abstract of the United States: 1969*
(90th edition), Washington, D.C., 1969; U.S. Bureau of the Census, *Historical Statistics
of the United States, Colonial Times to 1957: Continuation to 1962 and Revisions* (U.S.
Government Printing Office, Washington, D.C., 1965); *Congressional Quarterly Weekly
Report,* Vol. XXIV (1966), no. 45, p. 2809.

Note: While presenting these data I have not bothered to draw attention to the wide
range of errors that may exist. There are errors in collecting and recording data as well as
errors in computation. The Presidential election of 1960 provides an illustration of
another form of uncertainty that enters into these data—choices made among alternative
ways of presenting the data. It is customary to list the popular vote in such a way that
Kennedy appears a narrow winner over Nixon in 1960. Actually in order to reach this
distribution of the total vote it is necessary to exaggerate the Kennedy vote from
Alabama, since on the slate of Democratic electors in Alabama there were uncommitted
electors. Eventually six of the uncommitted electors voted for Harry Byrd; five electors
voted for Kennedy. If the Kennedy popular vote in Alabama is reduced to a proportion,
say 5/11 in this case, of the vote for Democratic electors and if only this reduced
popular vote is added to his national total, Nixon, not Kennedy, has the larger popular
vote total nationally in 1960. In percentages these are negligible changes, but symbolic-
ally such differences can become important. In these tables I have followed the usual
practice of presenting the augmented Kennedy total.

tional parties' candidates to vote for Wallace. The Congressional elections during the forty-year period illustrated in Figure 2.1 do not indicate the same degree of severe fluctuation; moreover, the path of Democratic percentages in Congressional elections is not closely associated with the Presidential elections. Figure 2.2 illustrates the important role played by the South in Democratic Party victories. The great advantage enjoyed there by the Democrats in Congressional elections has given them a lead of about 110 seats in the biennial contest for control of the House of Representatives in recent decades; the Democrats have frequently lost the popular vote contest in Congressional races in the North and still enjoyed a comfortable margin in Congress.

Figure 2.1 also illustrates the tendency of a victorious party in a Presidential election to do less well in the following Congressional election. From the Congressional vote in the Republican Presidential years of 1952 and 1956, we find an increase in the Democratic vote in 1954 and 1958. All the other Presidential elections in Figure 2.1 were Democratic victories, and in each succeeding Congressional election the Republican gained votes.

In analyzing Presidential and Congressional election data it is common to regard the Congressional vote as reflective of the underlying strength of the parties. The Republicans enjoyed a

FIGURE 2.2
Democratic Vote for Congressman, North and South, 1936-1968

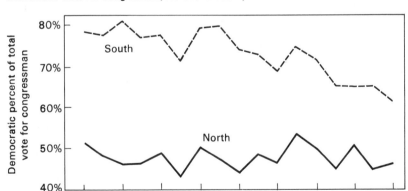

Source: Same as for Figure 2.1.

comeback in popularity in the late thirties and through much of the forties—a popularity which was not reflected in Presidential victories. During the fifties when the Republicans won the Presidency, their general strength in the electorate reflected through Congressional elections was declining.[1] Public opinion findings shown in Table 2.1 suggest the same pattern.

A somewhat different way of looking at this phenomenon follows from a comparison of the two lines in Figure 2.3. The voting behavior of independents in Figure 2.3 shows how much

FIGURE 2.3

Net Advantage between Republicans and Democrats in Presidential and Congressional Voting among Independents, 1952-1968

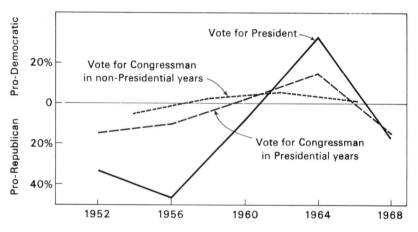

Source: Survey Research Center, University of Michigan.

they switch from election to election in their net impact of support of each party's candidates. We can also observe from this table that in most Presidential elections the independents swing strongly to one side or the other, and that this is one manifestation of the short-run forces at work in the electorate which benefit one candidate. Independents do not switch their support in Con-

[1] Philip Converse and the staff of the Survey Research Center have dealt with the problem of "normal" vote in a far more sophisticated way, employing party identification. For explanation of this technique see Angus Campbell et al., *Elections and the Political Order* (New York: John Wiley and Sons, 1966), pp. 9-39.

TABLE 2.1
The Party Identification of the Electorate, 1940-1968

	1940	1944	1947	1952	1954	1956	1958	1960	1962	1964	1966	1968
Democrats	41%	41%	46%	47%	47%	44%	47%	46%	47%	51%	45%	45%
Independents	20	20	21	22	22	24	19	23	23	22	28	29
Republicans	38	39	27	27	27	29	29	27	27	24	25	24
Nothing, Don't know	1	*	7	4	4	3	5	4	3	2	2	2
Total	100%	100%	101%	100%	100%	100%	100%	100%	100%	99%	100%	100%
n =[a]	?	?	1287	1614	1139	1772	1269	3021	1317	1571	1291	1558
	(Gallup)		(NORC)					(Survey Research Center)				

Sources: National Opinion Research Center; Survey Research Center, University of Michigan; George Gallup, *The Political Almanac, 1952* (New York: Forbes, 1952), p. 37; A. Campbell et al., *Elections and the Political Order,* p. 13.

[a]In this table and most of those which follow, the number of individuals interviewed is given underneath the total percentage for the column. In each table the "n's" give the number of individuals who are represented by the percentages in the column above. In this table the "n's" represent the total sample sizes of many studies, but in most tables the "n's" will represent subsets of a single sample.

gressional elections nearly as much as they do in Presidential elections. Beyond that we should note that in non-Presidential election years there is still less shifting in the net impact of independents' voting.

COMPETITIVENESS AND TURNOUT

To get a richer and different perspective on elections we need to keep in mind that almost all elections are conducted within small constituencies and that most elections in most constituencies are not closely contested. Although constituencies usually respond to general trends, most elections are rather one-sided and relatively few constituencies always have close elections. Even so, usually safe districts will become competitive in some elections when, say, a usually safe Republican district becomes closely contested in a strong Democratic year or a usually safe Democratic district swings so far in a Republican year that it becomes competitive. In the same way, of course, usually competitive constituencies become safe when partisan forces move them strongly in one direction. *Competitive districts shift support from party to party constantly, and although the magnitude of variation in these districts may not be greater than in others, it causes elections to be won and lost.* For this reason, small shifts in highly competitive districts may loom far more significant to politicians and journalists than do much larger variations in safer constituencies. Obviously this applies to states as the units in the electoral college, to Congressional districts, or to local constituencies.

The general tendency of constituencies to shift in the same direction should not be overemphasized. In every election some constituencies will move against the tide for special local reasons like an unusually strong or weak candidate or some exceptional issue. In a few elections large numbers of constituencies may move in opposite directions. Recently many Southern constituencies have moved in a Republican direction while the rest of the nation was voting more Democratic.

There is no agreed definition of "competitive," but sophisticated analysis takes into account the frequency of changeover from one party to another. A simpler definition is the winning margin in a single election. A highly competitive race is one in which the winner has less than 52 percent of the vote and the loser more than 48 percent. A marginal race is one in which the winner has less than 55 percent and the loser has more than 45 percent. More one-sided races are considered landslides or safe districts. *About one-half of Congressional districts in the United States remain safe for one party through both Democratic and Republican years.* In a single year, 1962, less than 20 percent of the races for the House of Representatives were competitive (that is, had a close election); in 1964 about 25 percent were competitive. In 1964, 45 percent of the United States Senate races were competitive, but this appears to be an atypically high rate for competitiveness, with most years having less than 40 percent of the contests closer than 55 to 45 percent. Furthermore, the amount of variation is not constant from district to district. Some districts appear immune to the forces influencing other districts, while some fluctuate so much that they appear safely Democratic in one election and safely Republican in another. Another source of variation to be considered below is the difference in turnout from one election to the next.

A most significant correlate of interest in politics is partisanship, and this relationship produces an important characteristic in national voting patterns. We have observed above that usually the party which lost the previous Presidential election gains in Congress in off-year elections. The most straightforward explanation of this regular phenomenon is that *Presidential elections with the accompanying high level of interest draw large numbers of weak partisans and independents to the polls.* These weak partisans and independents are more easily shifted from one party to another—they add disproportionately to the vote for one Presidential candidate—usually the winner. *In Congressional elections these less-committed voters do not turn out, and disproportionately large numbers of intense partisans vote in these less salient elections.* These strong party identifiers are not so likely to shift their vote away from their party as are other voters. Consequently in Congressional elections there is a decline in the support for the party that had disproportionately large numbers of less-interested voters in the previous Presidential elections. Even in hotly contested Congressional elections there will be high turnout among strong partisans and less turnout among the weak partisans and independents. In low-interest Congressional elections there are still greater differences in turnout. Primary elections further exaggerate this tendency. In all elections the less partisan voters represent a more shiftable group, voters more likely to shift for an attractive candidate or over an important issue.[2]

PARTISAN STABILITY

The discussion of voting to this point has emphasized variation, but the stable element in vote choice is equally important. During the past twenty years, while there have been landslide elections for both parties in Presidential and Congressional elections, party loyalty has remained almost unchanged. The general sympathy for, and identification with, the two political parties has shown remarkably little fluctuation during this period of considerable shifting in aggregate voting behavior.

Table 2.1 presents public opinion survey results from 1940 to 1968. By 1947 the present pattern of partisan preferences is established, while prior to that the shift away from the Republican Party occurred. (The 1940 and 1944 percentages for the Republicans appear somewhat exaggerated and the "apoliticals" underestimated.) Presumably this erosion of Republican strength began in the late 1920s, continuing with some variation through the thirties, but there are no survey data from that period to document this shifting for individuals. There are two sources of minor variation during this recent period of stability: one is the increase in numbers of Democrats; the other is the further decline in Republican strength. The basic distribution shows that the Democrats and Republicans were almost evenly balanced in the early forties. (With the lower level of turnout among Democrats this would lead to a Republican advantage in normal vote such as we observed in the Congressional elections of 1942 and 1946.) The distribution of the last fifteen years, however, shows a clear advantage to the Democrats with only slightly less than 50 percent of the electorate as Democrats and slightly over one-fourth as Republicans.

---

[2] These phenomena are discussed more thoroughly in Angus Campbell et al., *Elections and the Political Order*, pp. 40-62.

PARTISANSHIP

The pioneer studies in voting behavior ignored partisanship because the early emphasis was on social variables like religion and occupation. Since the first major study by Angus Campbell and his colleagues at the Survey Research Center in 1952,[3] party identification has assumed a central role in all voting behavior analysis. Party identification is a relatively uncomplicated measure which arrays responses to the following questions:

"Generally speaking, do you usually think of yourself as a Republican, a Democrat, an independent, or what? Would you call yourself a strong (R) (D) or a not very strong (R) (D)?"

> Strong Democrat
> Democrat
> Independent
> Republican
> Strong Republican

As this self-identification measure of party loyalty is the best indicator of partisanship, political analysts commonly refer to partisanship and party identification interchangeably. *Partisanship is the most important single influence on political opinions and voting behavior.* Many other influences are at work on voters in our society, but none compare in significance with partisanship.[4]

Partisanship represents the feeling of sympathy for, and loyalty to, a political party which an individual acquires (probably) during childhood and which endures (usually) with increasing intensity through his life. Since most individuals think of themselves as something politically, this self-image of oneself as a Democrat or a Republican is useful to the individual in a special way. An individual who thinks of himself as a Republican, for example, responds to political information in part by using his party identification to orient himself, to react to new information in such a way that it fits in with the ideals and feelings he already has. A Republican who hears a policy advocated by a Republican

[3] Angus Campbell, Gerald Gurin, and Warren Miller, *The Voter Decides* (Evanston: Row, Peterson and Co., 1954).

[4] The most important work on party identification is in Angus Campbell et al., *The American Voter* (New York: John Wiley and Sons, 1960), pp. 120-67.

Party leader has a basis in his party loyalty for supporting the policy quite apart from other considerations. Or a Democrat may feel favorable toward a candidate for office because he discovers that he is the Democratic candidate. Partisanship may orient the individual in his political environment, but it may also distort his picture of reality.

In order to refine slightly the categories of party identifiers shown in Table 2.1 in the following analysis, the individuals who have never voted are eliminated from the partisan and independent categories. These are the habitual non-voters discussed in chapter 1. This does not alter substantially the overall composition of the electorate as illustrated by Table 2.1, but it does change the characteristics of the groups by setting apart the habitual non-voters. This yields five categories of active participants in the electorate according to intensity of partisanship as follows:

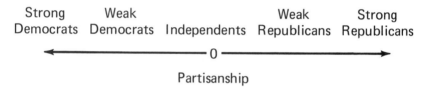

The partisans, strong Democrats and strong Republicans, are loyal to their party and likely to vote in all elections. The sympathizers, weak Democrats and weak Republicans, are less likely to vote and are more likely to desert their party occasionally for the other party. The independents have little or no loyalty to either party.

Figure 2.4 shows how these categories of voters behave in Presidential elections according to the findings of the five major Survey Research Center surveys. Strong Democratic and Republican partisans report a high degree of loyalty to their party's candidates over the years; naturally, almost no partisans have consistently voted for the other party and relatively few have ever switched. The independents, on the other hand, seldom vote consistently for one party—over 60 percent reporting in all surveys that they have voted for Presidential candidates from both parties.

Figure 2.5 shows another pattern of voting behavior among partisans and independents in the Presidential elections of 1952, 1956, 1960, 1964, and 1968. Overwhelmingly strong partisans support the candidate of their party, although there are obviously

FIGURE 2.4
Party Regularity in Presidential Voting for Partisans and Independents in 1952, 1956, 1960, 1964, and 1968

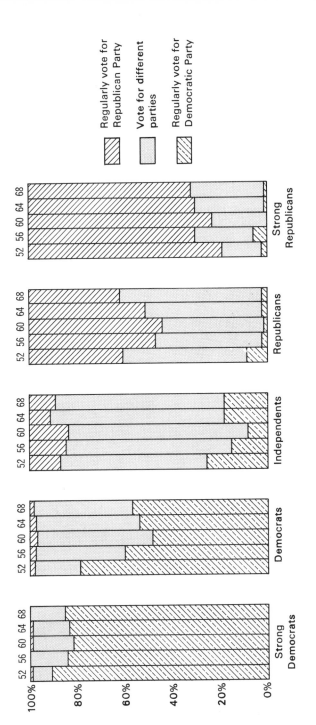

Regularly vote for
Republican Party

Vote for different
parties

Regularly vote for
Democratic Party

Source: Survey Research Center, University of Michigan.

39

FIGURE 2.5
Vote for President by Partisans and Independents in 1952, 1956, 1960, 1964, and 1968

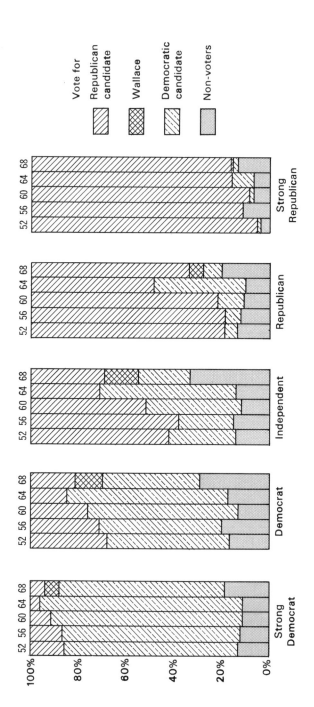

Source: Survey Research Center, University of Michigan.

differences in the appeal of candidates. Eisenhower received exceptionally large proportions of the vote in all categories from most Republican to most Democratic; Goldwater received exceptionally low proportions of the vote in all categories. The turnout varies somewhat in Presidential elections, revealing a slight tendency for the weak partisans to stay at home and a slight tendency for Democrats to stay at home more than the Republicans. (If individuals who never vote were added to these figures, the Democrats would appear to have even more non-voters; more habitual non-voters consider themselves Democrats than Republicans.)

In the perspective of party strategy these categories of voters must be approached with different purposes in mind. A party has these aims for the respective groups:

VOTER CATEGORY	PARTY STRATEGY
Partisans and sympathizers of the party	—hold their votes and maximize turnout
Independents	—try to win their support
Partisans and sympathizers of the opposition	—try to win their support or appeal to them enough to reduce their turnout
Habitual non-voters	—recruit new voters from potential supporters

It is difficult in practice to isolate these groups and apply a narrow strategy to one type of voter alone. Since political campaigners use appeals that are more or less appropriate for everyone, it might be more correct to say that a general campaign approach aims at rather dissimilar results in different categories of voters. *By making the party's platform and candidates attractive, the party intends to improve turnout and fund-raising among its followers, to win over independents, and at least to increase indifference to the choices among the opposition.*

PARTISANS

The highly stable patterns of party loyalty and political independence in Tables 2.2 and 2.3 are the basis of our description of the national electorate. Throughout this period, the Democrats hold a substantial advantage over the Republicans—an advantage which ranges from three to two in 1956 to a high of two to one in 1964. This means, among other things, that in the nation as a whole the Democratic Party begins a campaign with many more supporters than does the Republican Party. Broadly speaking, the Democrats must try to *hold onto* their following during a campaign, while the Republicans must try to *win over* a following.

TABLE 2.2
The Distribution of Partisans and Independents in 1952, 1956, 1960, 1964, and 1968

	1952	1956	1960	1964	1968
Strong Democrats	19%	19%	19%	25%	19%
Weak Democrats	21	20	22	23	23
Independents	19	21	19	18	25
Weak Republicans	12	13	13	13	14
Strong Republicans	13	14	14	11	9
Never voted	16	14	11	10	10
Total	100%	101%	98%	100%	100%
n =	1614	1762	1923	1440	1559

Source: Survey Research Center, University of Michigan.

   The advantage that the Democrats enjoy nationally is largely a result of the overwhelming majority of Democrats in the South, as shown in Table 2.3. If the South is disregarded where there are comparatively few independents and Republicans, the alignment of Democrats and Republicans outside the South is fairly evenly balanced. To an even greater degree *in the North, the independents hold the balance of power between Democrats and Republicans.* Furthermore the most one-sided distributions fall in 1964, reflecting a temporary abandonment of the Republican Party resulting from the Goldwater candidacy. In both 1964 and in 1968 the Republicans failed to gain support not only in the North but also in the South, where their strategy predicted great gains. It is difficult to anticipate whether or not the increase in proportions of independents will continue.

TABLE 2.3
The Distribution of Partisans and Independents for the South and Non-South in 1952, 1956, 1960, 1964, and 1968

	SOUTH					NON-SOUTH				
	1952	1956	1960	1964	1968	1952	1956	1960	1964	1968
Strong Democrats	24%	24%	22%	33%	24%	17%	17%	18%	22%	16%
Weak Democrats	21	25	29	26	24	21	18	19	21	22
Independents	8	12	13	11	25	24	25	23	22	26
Weak Republicans	4	6	8	7	7	15	15	16	16	17
Strong Republicans	5	6	11	8	4	17	17	17	12	11
Never voted	38	26	18	15	16	7	8	7	8	8
Total	100%	99%	101%	100%	100%	101%	100%	100%	101%	100%
n =	433	513	645	443	481	1140	1247	1278	997	1076

Source: Survey Research Center, University of Michigan

43

INDEPENDENTS

The independents are the most obvious source of additional votes for either party, given the composition of the national electorate. While loyal supporters of a party sometimes abandon it, as when Democrats voted for Eisenhower in large numbers or when Republicans voted for Johnson in preference to Goldwater, year after year the largest bloc of voters available to both parties is the independents. Table 2.2 shows that independents account for about one-fifth of the national electorate, and Table 2.4 indicates the independent's capacity for shifting back and forth between the major parties. In recent years each party has successfully appealed to the independents on occasion, winning over a large majority to its side. In 1968 a sizable proportion gave its votes to Wallace.

TABLE 2.4
The Distribution of Votes for President by Independents from 1940 to 1968

	1940	1944	1948	1952	1956	1960	1964	1968
Democratic	61%	62%	57%	33%	27%	46%	66%	32%
Republican	39	38	43	67	73	54	34	47
Wallace (1968)								21
Total	100%	100%	100%	100%	100%	100%	100%	100%
n =	?	?	?	263	309	298	219	228
		(Gallup Poll)			(Survey Research Center)			

Source: George Gallup, *The Political Almanac, 1952*, p. 38; and Survey Research Center, University of Michigan.

It is appropriate to inquire on what basis the independents switch their party preferences. One of the contentions of the major voting studies has been that the popular view of political independents as intelligent, informed, dispassionate evaluators of candidates, parties, and issues is mistaken. Studies from the Bureau of Applied Social Research and the Survey Research Center have supported the view that partisans of both parties are better informed and more concerned with politics than are the independents. This analysis has been reflected recently in the campaign strategies of both Democratic and Republican organizations. Increasingly the view has become that the available voters, the voters that can be won over to either party, are an uninformed, apathetic group in whom intelligent appeals to issues and reasoned debate would be lost. (Some differences in perspective are involved here. If one is concerned only with the individuals in the electorate who have not made a choice between Presidential candidates, say, by the last two weeks of the campaign, they are indeed an uninformed, apathetic lot and it is difficult to find any basis for their eventual vote choice. If, on the other hand, one is concerned with all the individuals who are available to both parties sometime between one election and the next or who switch preferences between elections, they are not at all uninformed and apathetic in comparison with standpat voters.)[5]

The case against the independents has been overstated. It is true that independents are not as interested in campaigns or as concerned with which candidate wins as are strong partisans, a pattern shown in Figure 2.6. The possibility exists, however, that these measures of "high interest" in the campaign and "great concern" with the outcome of the election are tapping the enthusiasm of the partisans for their party's Presidential candidate rather than for a more general interest in politics. Nonetheless Figure 2.6 does demonstrate the consistent lack of concern and interest among weak partisans and independents in Presidential campaigns and elections. This is a partial explanation of why it is so difficult to get the attention of the American public during even the most exciting political campaigns. The evidence of general interest in politics shown in Table 2.5 shows no relationship between partisans and independents and not a particularly high interest in politics within any group.

With other indicators of interest and involvement in politics the same pattern emerges. In the level of ideological conceptualization, or seeing parties and candidates in ideological perspective, there are no differences between partisans and independents. The only difference is between Republicans and Democrats; Republicans with their higher level of education are more likely to view politics ideologically. On a sense of political efficacy, that is, how significantly one views his political activities, the same results

---

[5] The most extensive analysis of this point is in V. O. Key, Jr., *The Responsible Electorate* (Cambridge, Mass.: Belknap Press of Harvard University Press, 1966).

FIGURE 2.6
Interest among Partisans and Independents in 1952, 1956, 1960, 1964, and 1968

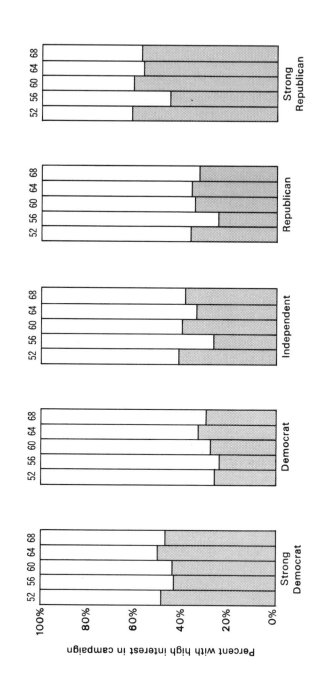

Source: Survey Research Center, University of Michigan.

obtain: there are no differences between independents and partisans, but Republicans have a higher sense of political efficacy than
Democrats.

TABLE 2.5
**Distribution of Interest in Government and Politics Generally according to Partisanship,
1968**

Interested	Strong Demo- crat	Weak Demo- crat	Inde- pendent	Weak Repub- lican	Strong Repub- lican
All the time	29%	23%	32%	29%	34%
Some of the time	28	25	27	26	30
Only now and then	14	16	17	19	16
Hardly at all	15	21	10	14	11
NA	13	15	14	12	9
Total	99%	100%	100%	100%	100%
n =	312	394	452	224	148

Source: Survey Research Center, University of Michigan.

It is surprising that with all the political survey research no
satisfactory measure of political information has been developed.
It has never been ascertained how well informed different
participants are. It is possible, as a substitute for a measure of
political information, to report whether or not individuals have
opinions on issues and make the assumption that the individuals
who have no opinions are poorly informed. Again using this
measure, there are no differences between partisans and independents, so by this test there is no basis for saying independents are
less well informed than are partisans, using our definitions of
independent and partisan.

The most nearly correct view of the independent, I believe, is
that independents are not much interested in politics and
government and certainly not much concerned with partisan
politics—they are not emotionally involved in party clashes. On
the other hand, independents appear to have the information and
the perspective on political affairs necessary for an evaluation of
issues and candidates as competent as could be expected of
partisans. Independents are no wiser or more virtuous than
partisans; nor are they less so. It is not clear whether their lack of

involvement means that independents are not easily aroused by political problems demanding their attention or whether their lack of involvement simply means that independents are less biased by partisan predispositions. This uncertainty is troublesome because independents may not be sufficiently motivated to play the role of intelligently mediating disputes between Democrats and Republicans. On the other hand, the self-perception of playing this mediating role may motivate independents effectively.

SHIFTING PARTISAN SYMPATHY

As most individuals never alter their partisan loyalties, this stability in party followers extends over generations. Very few individuals—less than 2 percent ordinarily—report a change in party identification in the period of a single year. The net gain or loss to one party in a single year is almost always under 1 percent. *Since 1936 the shifting of party loyalty has worked to the advantage of the Republicans.* Although some individuals in the electorate are moving away from the Republican Party, more are moving toward it. When we combine this characteristic with the pro-Democratic leanings of new members of the electorate, we find that the Democrats are gradually becoming more numerous and Republicans less numerous. *The advantage that Democrats enjoy among new voters more than offsets the losses to the Republicans among older voters.*

It is obviously much easier to change the preferences of voters in particular elections than to alter their basic partisan loyalties. The capacity that the electorate has demonstrated to shift support from one party to another is essential if there is to be a believable threat to political officeholders. If voting patterns were as stable as partisanship, officeholders would be relatively secure once elected. In fact, during recent decades Americans have varied their voting patterns greatly while providing the parties with a stable base of underlying loyalty which the parties could usually count on when entering electoral contests. On this score, the American electorate appears changeable enough nationally to prevent political leaders from taking the public for granted and stable enough to provide both political parties with an effective base of power from which to threaten the other party.

3

Social Characteristics of Partisans and Independents

To this point I have discussed the voting behavior and political partisanship of Americans without trying to explain these patterns. The major attempts to explain American voting behavior have relied on social and economic factors to account for both stability and change in American politics. The major studies of the Survey Research Center have documented a wide range of relationships in the American electorate between social and economic characteristics and political behavior. Furthermore, social and economic factors form the basis of many descriptions of voting patterns in American journalism and party strategies. Analysis regularly attributes political trends to a "farm revolt" or "fixed-income groups"; frequently these explanations rely on so-called bloc voting like "the black vote," "the Catholic vote," "the union vote," which imply at least that some social factor causes large numbers of people to vote the same way.

One persistently interesting and convenient way to describe political patterns is by regional distribution of partisans and by the size of the community in which they live. Even casual political commentary tries to distinguish Southern patterns from the rest of the country, and within regions often refers to "the city vote" or "the rural vote." Table 3.1 shows the actual regional and community size composition of strong Democratic and strong Republican partisans for the nation. As we saw earlier, the Democrats are disproportionately strong in the South, with

Southern Democrats accounting for 40 percent of all Democrats. The remaining Democrats are fairly evenly spread through the other three regions. Within the regions there are some basic differences between Republicans and Democrats. In the South the Democratic strength is in the towns and rural areas, while the other major Democratic concentrations are in the cities of the East and the towns of the Midwest. The Northern Democratic Party is disproportionately urban in contrast to the Southern wing of the party.

TABLE 3.1

The Composition of Strongly Partisan Democrats and Republicans according to Region and Community Size in 1968

		Strong Democrats		Strong Republicans
South	40%		14%	
Cities		10%		2%
Towns		15		4
Rural		15		8
East	22		30	
Cities		12		6
Towns		8		12
Rural		2		12
Midwest	25		35	
Cities		8		7
Towns		11		20
Rural		6		8
Far West	13		21	
Cities		5		8
Towns		5		8
Rural		3		5
Total	100%	100%	100%	100%
n =		294		142

Source: Survey Research Center, University of Michigan.

The Republican Party, on the other hand, is disproportionately a small town and medium-sized city party. The main regional bias in the Republican distribution is Midwest strength, and in the Midwest Republicans are likely to be in towns. In order not to give the impression that this represents a political description of these areas, it should be pointed out that *Democrats outnumber Republicans in every category* in Table 3.1 *except in the rural areas of the East.* These patterns have remained relatively stable in the last several decades except for the general decline in rural population.

POLITICAL AND SOCIAL CHARACTERISTICS

Frequently social descriptions turn to education and family income, occupation of head of household, race, and religion. The social characteristics of partisans and independents indicate that in most ways independents look like Republicans. Their levels of education and income are very similar, and the proportions of individuals from professional and managerial households are about 30 percent, almost identical among Republicans and independents. The proportion from manual workers' households among independents, about 40 percent, is closer to the proportion among Democrats. Independents are high in both these occupational categories because they have very low proportions among farmers and retired members of the electorate. Democrats are much more likely than Republicans to come from manual laborers' households and much less likely to come from white-collar households.

Democrats and independents are disproportionately Catholic, although there are not great differences in the religious composition of the various political categories. The differences in racial composition are somewhat greater, with about one-fifth of the strong Democrats being black, while only 1 percent of the strong Republicans are black. The majority of strong Democrats have not graduated from high school, but there are increasingly higher levels of education among each of the other categories as one moves toward the strong Republicans. Farmers are a very small proportion of each category, although the political strength of rural areas is based on more than farm households, since many individuals who do not farm live in rural areas.

The main conclusion to draw is that *on most social characteristics Democrats, Republicans, and independents are very heterogeneous.* On most characteristics there are substantial proportions all along the partisan dimension representing a mixed social composition in each category. There are poor Republicans and wealthy Democrats. There are urban Republicans and small-town Democrats; manual laborers are Republicans; doctors and lawyers are Democrats. There are Catholic Republicans, Southern Republicans, poorly educated Republicans, and a few black Republicans, just as there are well-educated Democrats, Midwestern Democrats, and Protestant Democrats. In all cases the tendency runs the other way, but these tendencies and their importance should not be exaggerated.

Socially mixed political groups mean that successful political appeals have been made in the past across social divisions and that social opportunities exist for future political appeals and growth in areas of current weakness. Socially mixed political groups are evidence of many years of political pluralism, of years of relatively non-doctrinaire political parties appealing to voters where they could find them.

Many of the social groupings which appear quite Democratic in the 1960s have also had periods of Republican loyalty. Some Catholics, particularly Italian Catholics, blacks, some Jewish groups, to mention only a few current Democratic strongholds, have been Republican in earlier periods. These old loyalties die hard and provide a basis for continuing to appeal to these groups. Another source of political variation in social groups is the possibility of a group's being Democratic in one community and Republican in another. Adding together these local differences creates an overall pattern of political variation.

A different way to investigate the distribution of partisans and independents is shown in Figure 3.1. By controlling for certain characteristics, starting with region and race, and where group size permits controlling in addition on religion and occupation, the partisan distributions of thirteen groupings are presented for 1968. There is a clear Democratic advantage in most groupings. The well-known Democratic dominance over Republicans in the South appears in the distributions of blacks and in all occupational categories among whites. Only the upper socioeconomic group has deviated from the basic Southern pattern of Democratic loyalty; the white-collar grouping is noticeably less strong as Democratic partisans and is more independent. In the North what might be called the "minority groups," the blacks, Jews, and Catholics, are heavily pro-Democratic. The manual workers among both Catholics and Protestants are pro-

FIGURE 3.1

Partisan Groupings in 1968 according to Region, Race, Religion, and Occupation[a]

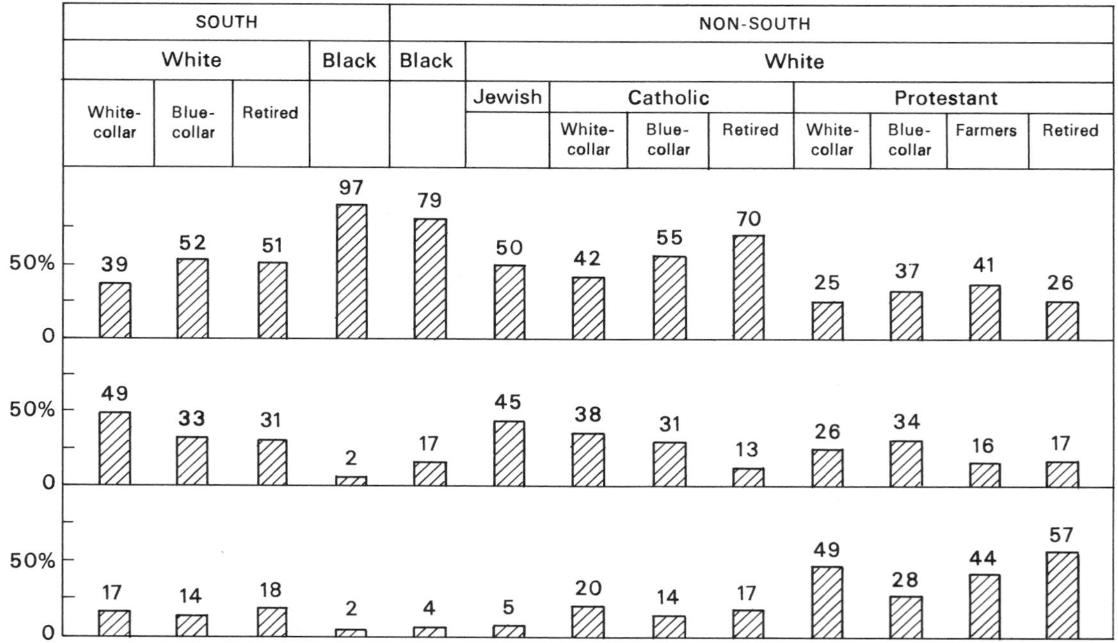

Source: Survey Research Center, University of Michigan.

[a]These categories account for 82% of the electorate in 1968, and no category which accounts for more than 2% is excluded from the table.

Democratic, although Catholic manual laborers are considerably more Democratic than are the Protestant manual laborers. Retired Catholics and blue-collar Catholics reveal strong pro-Democratic loyalties, while the Jewish grouping and the white-collar Catholics are less likely to be strongly partisan and more likely to be independents. The Republicans enjoy a clear advantage in partisan loyalty in only two groupings, the white-collar category and the retired category among Northern white Protestants. Independents are numerous in several groupings, particularly among Jews and white-collar Catholics, and for the first time in 1968 independents are numerous in the South. There is no particular social haven of independents.

Several distinctive political patterns in the American electorate are partially revealed by these configurations of data. The retired Catholics and retired Protestants are more strongly partisan than are other Catholics and Protestants; this is a reflection of the overall tendency in the electorate for the older members of society to be more partisan than are the young. The strength of identification with a party increases the more years that one holds the identification. Also, the data used in Figure 3.1 shows that individuals in farm households are more likely to be weak partisans regardless of which party they support. This is a reflection of the tendency of farmers to be extremely unstable in their voting patterns and to shift their partisan support more easily and more often than do other members of the electorate. Their weaker commitment to the parties facilitates swings in voting and leads to greater variation in turnout. Some observers argue that these traits of farmers increase their political power because candidates appeal to them disproportionately on the chance that they may benefit from the farmers' capacity to shift large numbers of votes.

During the sixteen years for which there is appropriate national survey data, the distributions within these groupings are remarkably stable, just as the overall distributions of party identification are stable for the same period. There are two substantial changes. One is the decline of permanent non-voters in the South, which has increased the proportions in all the partisan categories but has left Democratic dominance unchanged. The other change is among Northern white Protestants, where from 1952 to 1968 Republican strength increased among farmers and the retired, an increase of 15 percent in each group.

SOCIAL COMPOSITION OF POLITICAL GROUPINGS

There are advantages in looking at essentially the same data in a different way, since it is also possible to examine the social characteristics of political categories. To simplify the analysis, Table 3.2 shows only strong Democrats, independents, and strong Republicans. This form of analysis shows the social characteristics

TABLE 3.2
The Composition of Strong Partisans and Independents in 1968 according to Region, Race, Religion, and Occupation

	Strong Democrats	Independents	Strong Republicans
	SOUTH		
White			
White-collar	14%	48%	15%
Blue-collar	18	21	35
Farmer	4	2	5
Retired	17	17	30
Black	38	1	5
NA (on one or more items)	9	11	10
Total	100%	100%	100%
n =	117	121	20
	NON-SOUTH		
White			
Protestant			
White-collar	11%	20%	34%
Blue-collar	12	25	16
Farmer	2	2	3
Retired	7	5	20
Catholic			
White-collar	11	16	7
Blue-collar	10	11	4
Retired	8	1	2
Jewish	7	6	—
Black	18	4	1
NA (on one or more items)	14	10	13
Total	100%	100%	100%
n =	177	275	122

Source: Survey Research Center, University of Michigan.

of partisans and independents in the South and non-South. Such a presentation helps to avoid drawing incorrect conclusions about the composition of our political groupings. For example, even though Jews in the North are strongly pro-Democratic, they are so few in number that they account for less than 10 percent of all Democrats. White-collar Protestants in the North are unlikely to be Democrats, but they are so numerous generally that they rank among the largest categories.

Several basic points should be made about the political groupings. First, in the North and in the South Democrats are more diverse socially than Republicans, with white-collar and blue-collar households contributing substantially to their ranks, as well as a sizable bloc of blacks. In the South the independents are most likely to be white-collar whites with a noticeable minority of blue-collar workers; and, while Southern Republicans are similar socially, they are not so dependent on white-collar workers and are more dependent on retired people, who are frequently migrants. Outside the South a remarkably similar picture emerges, with the Democrats composed of several different social groups, in contrast to the Republicans who are again disproportionately from white-collar Protestant households. Northern Republicans also have a concentration of retired white Protestants. Northern independents are not unlike Northern Democrats in social composition except that very few independents are blacks.

Table 3.2 not only shows how effective the political parties have been in appealing to various social groups, it also shows that both parties depend on a range of social groupings for their electoral strength. To put this differently, the political parties have the stable loyalties of socially diverse groups and have a strong incentive to retain these faithful supporters by continuing to appeal to them, since it is easier to maintain partisanship than to win converts. This incentive in both major political parties deters a political stand that would drastically realign the parties socially.

SOCIAL GROUP ANALYSIS

Social analysis of political behavior has depended mainly on three units: primary groups, secondary groups, and social classes. Briefly these terms have the following meanings: primary groups are the face-to-face groups one associates with, like family, friends, and fellow workers; secondary groups are organizations or collections of individuals with whom one identifies or is identified but are too large to meet with personally; social classes are broad groupings of social positions in society according to status. Not particularly abstract analytic concepts, their explanatory power depends on common social experiences and circumstances.

PRIMARY GROUPS

The impact of social groups on individual behavior is so commonplace that it needs little elaboration, and the forms of group influence are too varied to discuss them all. First, primary groups will be considered. Although investigations of the political behavior of primary groups are not numerous, *all available evidence indicates that families and groups of friends are very likely to be politically homogeneous.* Groups of workers appear somewhat more mixed politically. Presumably the social forces in families and friendship groups are more intense and more likely to be based on, or to result in, political unanimity, but in most work situations people are thrown together without an opportunity to self-select themselves into groups by common political values or on any other basis. At least friendship groups, even casual ones, may be formed in such ways that individuals with much in common—including political views—naturally come together.

Table 3.3 reproduces a set of findings originally presented by Campbell, Converse, Miller, and Stokes in *The American Voter* from their 1952 national survey. These data on the voter's primary groups do not reflect the indecisiveness of some voters or the extent to which primary groups have mixed preferences or the voting preferences are unknown. Nevertheless, where an individual is aware of a partisan preference, that preference is extremely likely to correspond with his own.

We have avoided the word *conformity* to describe this pattern of primary group behavior because these group processes are more casual and more a matter of give-and-take than *conformity* implies. Most people care very little about politics, and it plays a small part in their personal relations. In very few primary groups is politics of any consequence, so the things which happen

TABLE 3.3

Relation of Reported Partisan Preference of Primary Groups to Respondent's Own Partisan Choice, 1952[a]

RESPONDENT VOTED	SPOUSE VOTED		FAMILY VOTED[b]		FRIENDS VOTED		WORK ASSOCIATES VOTED	
	Dem.	Rep.	Dem.	Rep.	Dem.	Rep.	Dem.	Rep.
Democratic	89%	7%	80%	8%	83%	15%	79%	24%
Republican	11	93	20	92	85	85	21	76
Total	100%	100%	100%	100%	100%	100%	100%	100%
n[c] =	337	496	75	108	355	574	271	290

Source: Angus Campbell et al., *The American Voter* (New York: John Wiley and Sons, 1960), p. 77, Table 4.3.

[a] This tabulation is limited to persons who reported voting for a major-party candidate for President and who could attribute to the primary group in question a clear partisan preference.

[b] Asked only of unmarried respondents.

[c] Includes a small number of persons who voted for a minor-party candidate.

in the group that lead to political homogeneity are of low salience. One gradually creates and revises an image of the world and evaluations of that image through social pressures, many of these processes being face-to-face exchanges of information or reassurances that someone else shares views or considers them plausible, realistic, acceptable. Most individuals are not "pressured" by primary groups to conform or to change politically, at least not nearly so much as they influence one another casually by expressing the same ideas and values without even thinking about it. Ordinarily primary groups do not tolerate high levels of political tension and conflict. Also very few people are subject to the social forces of only one or two primary groups, so conformity to group pressure would mean conformity to a large number of groups.

In addition to what happens within primary groups, there is another factor that produces political similarity: the likelihood that primary group members share the same social background and experiences outside the group. *It is most probable that members of any primary group are socially, economically, ethnically, racially alike, and being alike in these ways means that the same general social influences are at work on them.* Much happens outside the primary group to make it politically homogenous.

SECONDARY GROUPS

"Secondary groups" refers to the level of social organization between primary groups and social classes. This covers a range of groups and groupings in society like labor unions, religious organizations, and occupational groupings. *Secondary groups are presumably composed of networks of overlapping primary groups where pressures toward political homogeneity spill over and tend to make the members of secondary groups alike.* In addition the members of secondary groups are likely to be subject to the same social forces outside the group. For example, members of a labor union are likely to be in the same income group, to live in the same type of neighborhood, and to have the same social and educational background, all of which would tend to make them alike politically.

A third factor at work is the role a secondary group may play as a reference group. A group serves as a reference group for an individual if he uses the group as a guide in forming opinions. For example, if a union member identifies with his labor union and he perceives that a particular policy is good for his union and if he favors the policy because of the perceived advantage to his union, then the union is a political reference group for the individual. In the same way, if a union member believes that other union members support a policy and if he supports the policy in part for this reason, the union members serve as a reference group. Also, if a white-collar worker perceives that unions favor a policy and he opposes it in part for that reason, the union serves as a negative reference group for him.

The most sophisticated analysis of social groups and political behavior applied to national survey data appears in *The American Voter.*[1] The authors demonstrated a distinctive influence on political behavior attributed to secondary membership among union members, blacks, Catholics, and Jews by controlling on many outside social influences with matched groups. They were

---

[1] Angus Campbell et al., *The American Voter* (New York: John Wiley and Sons, 1960), pp. 295-332.

able to show that these groups except for Catholics were considerably more Democratic than one would expect from the group members' other social characteristics, such as urban-rural residence, region, and occupation status. These findings from *The American Voter* are shown in Table 3.4, and the positive figures represent the additional pro-Democratic influence on individuals supplied by particular group memberships.

TABLE 3.4
Distinctiveness of Presidential Vote among Certain Groups, with Life Situation Controlled, 1956[a]

	1956 PRESIDENTIAL VOTE
Members of union households	+17.1
Union members	+20.4
Catholics	+ 2.9
Blacks	
Non-South	+11.6
South	+15.4
Jews	+45.4

Source: Angus Campbell et al., *The American Voter* (New York: John Wiley and Sons, 1960), p. 306, Table 12.2.

[a]The entry in each cell represents a deviation in percent Democratic of the two-party vote within the test group from a comparable percent computed for control groups matched with the test groups for a variety of conditions of life situation.

Even greater influence is present if the individual identifies with the group. In order to establish the importance of identification with the group and belief in the legitimacy of the group's involvement in politics, the distributions of union members, blacks, Catholics, and Jews in Table 3.5 were presented in *The American Voter.* The increasing impact of identification and perceived legitimacy is demonstrated by the increasing magnitude of the Democratic percentages moving from the lower right-hand corner of Table 3.5 up and to the left. *The stronger the belief in legitimacy and the stronger the group identification, the greater the impact of group standards.*

TABLE 3.5

Presidential Vote across Four Secondary Membership Groups with Democratic Voting Standards, by Strength of Group Identification and Belief in Legitimacy of Group Political Activity, 1956[a] (Survey Research Center, University of Michigan)

	GROUP IDENTIFICATION			
Belief in Legitimacy of Group Political Activity	High	Medium	Low	Total
Strong	72%	64%	55%	65%
Medium	62%	55%	45%	53%
Weak	67%	45%	33%	41%
Total	69%	56%	43%	

Source: Angus Campbell et al., *The American Voter* (New York: John Wiley and Sons, 1960), p. 322, Table 12.8.

[a] Each cell entry represents the percent Democratic of the two-party vote for the appropriate combination of group identification and sense of legitimacy. The "Total" column shows the simple relationship between legitimacy and the vote, with no control on identification. The "Total" row shows the simple relationship between identification and the vote, without control on legitimacy.

For all that, in American society large secondary groups are politically heterogeneous. Apparently even these pro-Democratic secondary groups are made up of dissimilar primary groups; to some extent the members are subject to dissimilar social forces. Possibly the significance of secondary groups would appear greater if they were investigated in a narrower, more limited way, rather than aggregated nationally. Essentially, this is what the original community voting studies from the Bureau of Applied Research at Columbia University did in Erie County and Elmira.[2] Looking at secondary groups in a single community, they found that these group memberships explained a large part of the observed political opinions and voting behavior. Certainly many politicians operate as if local secondary groups were politically homogeneous, and national data cannot dismiss this possibility.

[2] The serious student of political behavior must consider these studies, but we will slight them in this introduction because it has proved difficult to translate their findings directly into national patterns. The 1940 study of Erie County is reported in Paul Lazarsfeld, Bernard Berelson, and Hazel Gaudet, *The People's Choice*; the 1948 Elmira study is reported in Bernard Berelson, Paul Lazarsfeld, and William McPhee, *Voting*.

RELIGION AND VOTING BEHAVIOR

Usually the voting patterns of American religious groups are not particularly distinctive, or at least other factors are considered more important in determining vote choice. The 1960 Presidential election provides a good example of how secondary groups become relevant in a particular election and temporarily have great influence on voting behavior. Kennedy's Catholicism was a major issue throughout the campaign and of great salience to both Catholics and non-Catholics.

The Survey Research Center researchers separated Protestant Democrats according to the frequency with which they attend church and compared each group's defection from Kennedy by calculating the normal defection of the group. Figure 3.2 shows their findings. In both the South and North those who are more regular in church attendance are more likely to defect from the Catholic candidate. Among the nominal Protestants who never attend church, Kennedy's Catholicism had no such impact.

Although the evidence is meager on this point, political analysts believe that the temporary salience of the religious issue in 1960 and the sharper drawing of social lines around religious boundaries is typical of what happens to many social factors occasionally. *A social factor like religion or union membership or Italian ancestry or wheat farming will become important temporarily during a political campaign after years of low salience, and will become unimportant subsequently.* This irregular rising and falling of issues dramatizing social groups is another partial explanation for the political heterogeneity of American social groups. If the issues that dramatize a given social group were constantly salient, there would eventually be a pure partisan realignment of the group. But if the group is politically salient for only one campaign or so, such major realignment does not occur. Presumably, as such issues are raised, there is a slight partisan realignment, but the changing salience of groups leads to political heterogeneity rather than to pure divisions.

SOCIAL CLASSES

The third major unit of analysis is social class. Some of the leading hypotheses of social and political theory link social classes and

FIGURE 3.2
Defection to Nixon among Protestant Democrats as a Function of Church Attendance[a]
(Survey Research Center, University of Michigan)

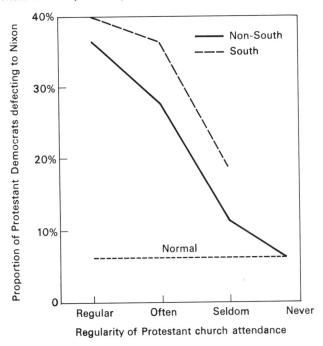

Source: Angus Campbell et al., *Elections and the Political Order* (New York: John Wiley and Sons, 1966) p. 89, Figure 5.1.
[a]The number of Protestant Democrats who "never" attend church in the South is too small for inclusion.

political behavior. Generally the expectations surrounding social class include these: (1) that there are social differences in economic and social interests, and (2) that these conflicting interests which follow social class lines will be translated into political forces. The critical variable in this view appears to be the salience of social class interests, and *in American society the importance of social class fluctuates but never becomes extremely high.* The major political and sociological theories of social class have taken for granted the supreme importance of class interests, but this assumption seems unrealistic in American society. About one-third of all American adults say that they never think of themselves as members of a social class.

A majority of Americans are able to place themselves in a general social position if given a choice between "middle class" and "working class" and even "upper" or "lower" within a class. Even though the individual self-ratings are not perfectly congruent with the positions that social analysts would assign them on the basis of characteristics like occupation, income, and education, a general social class structure does exist. The political significance of social class has been shown to vary by the authors of *The American Voter* in much the same way as for secondary groups. Figure 3.3 from *The American Voter* shows the correlations which indicate the strength of the relationship between social class and vote choice in four elections. The correlations in parentheses mean

FIGURE 3.3
Status Polarization of Presidential and Congressional Votes, 1944-1956 (Survey Research Center, University of Michigan for the 1948, 1952, and 1956 data; National Opinion Research Center for the 1944 data)

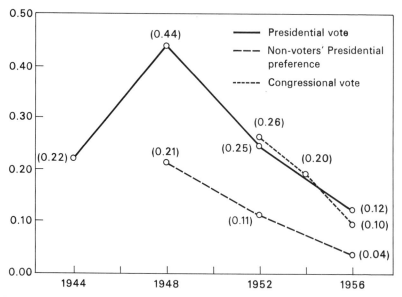

Source: Angus Campbell et al., *The American Voter* (New York: John Wiley and Sons, 1960), p. 347, Figure 3.2.

The points shown represent degree of relationship measured by tau$_b$ between the occupation status of non-farm respondents and their partisan vote or preference.

that in the 1948 Presidential election there was a much stronger relationship between vote choice and social class than in the elections immediately before and after. It is not permissible to infer that social class necessarily caused vote choices in these elections but simply that in 1948 large proportions of middle-class voters supported Dewey, the Republican candidate, and large proportions of working-class voters supported Truman. Or, to describe the pattern a different way, in 1944, 1952, and 1956 there were not substantial differences in the support for Roosevelt and Eisenhower among middle-class and working-class voters. These same patterns of low relationship continue through 1960, 1964, and 1968.

However, these relationships can be accounted for by the presence of differing numbers of partisans in the social class categories. Or, to put it differently, middle-class respondents appear more conservative because more Republicans are in the middle-class categories and Republicans are conservative. Working-class individuals appear more liberal because there are proportionally more liberal Democrats in the working class. Furthermore, middle-class Democrats are just as liberal as working-class Democrats, while working-class Republicans are about as conservative as middle-class Republicans. Actually *there is some variation associated with social class that is independent of partisanship, but the relationship with partisanship is much stronger.* Social class may serve as a political guide for some citizens on certain issues, but it does not appear to be extremely important in American politics. As much as anything else, this is a reflection of the tendency of political leaders not to emphasize highly divisive social class issues.

Next to Canada the United States is usually regarded as an extreme case among developed democracies for the insignificance of social class in political behavior; in most European democracies social class is of greater consequence.[3] Two factors may depress the apparent relationship between social class and voting behavior

---

[3] There are several important works on social class and political behavior in addition to *The American Voter,* chap. 13. Students interested in this area of analysis should see Robert Alford, *Party and Society* (Chicago: Rand McNally and Company, 1963) and Heinz Eulau, *Class and Party in the Eisenhower Years* (New York: The Free Press, 1962). Perhaps the most significant work is David Butler and Donald E. Stokes, *Political Change in Britain* (New York: St. Martin's Press, 1969).

in the United States. Aggregating data for the entire population may cover up stronger relationships for subgroups and in particular communities. Furthermore, American political leaders make broad appeals intended to cross and disrupt social class lines. One interpretation of American political history portrays the twentieth century in terms of suppressing class issues and making politics unimportant for, and uninteresting to, the lower social classes.[4]

SOCIAL CROSS PRESSURES

One of the major concerns of the early voting studies by Lazarsfeld, Berelson, and other researchers at the Bureau of Applied Social Research of Columbia University was the "cross pressure hypothesis." This perspective will be used to examine some short-run and long-run influence on political acts. The cross pressure hypothesis is simple in outline, but it can be confusing because it takes so many different forms. The hypothesis is based on the existence of two (or more) forces or tendencies, one in a Republican direction and the other in a Democratic direction. Sometimes this is stated as two factors *predisposing* a voter in a Republican or a Democratic direction. Usually the hypothesis is presented with two social dimensions like occupation and religion:

	White-collar	Blue-collar
Occupation:	←	→
	Pro-Republican	Pro-Democratic
	Protestant	Catholic
Religion:	←	→
	Pro-Republican	Pro-Democratic

Some individuals are *predisposed* or pushed in a consistent way such as white-collar Protestants with both occupation and religion predisposing them in a Republican direction or blue-collar Catholics predisposed in a Democratic direction.

[4] The major argument is made by E. E. Schattschneider, *The Semisovereign People*.

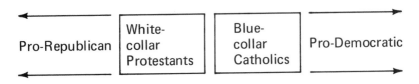

But some individuals are predisposed in both directions or "cross pressured."

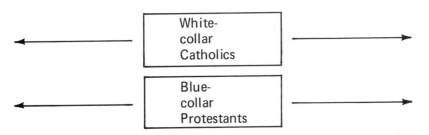

The cross pressure hypothesis asserts that the individuals who are under consistent pressure behave differently from individuals under cross pressure. The predictions under the hypothesis are:

CONSISTENT PRESSURE
straight ticket voting
early decision on vote
high interest in politics
high levels of information
consistent attitudes

CROSS PRESSURE
split ticket voting
late decision on vote
low interest in politics
low levels of information
conflicting attitudes

These expectations about voting behavior under cross pressure are actually specific applications of more general patterns investigated by sociologists and psychologists in a variety of ways. The responses to cross pressure predicted by the hypothesis are avoidance reactions—efforts to avoid or to minimize the anxiety produced by conflict.

CROSS PRESSURE AND POLITICAL THEORY

There is another application associated with the cross pressure thesis in empirical political theory. Many large social groups are expected to be stable politically according to the cross pressure hypothesis, i.e., they are consistently predisposed to be Republican or Democratic by the social forces working on them, and therefore social pressures which consistently predispose voters lead to political stability among both Republicans and Democrats because they have politically consistent social backgrounds.

Between these politically consistent social groups there are cross pressured groups predisposed toward both parties and according to the cross pressure thesis these groups are politically unstable. These cross pressured groups provide the voters who switch from one party to another, and this means that the available voters, the voters to whom the parties must appeal in order to win new voters, are in a position between Democrats and Republicans. Consequently, the argument goes, these available voters have social and political attitudes somewhere between Republicans and Democrats. Furthermore, the politically unstable social base means that these voters are easily switched from one party to another, so they are sensitive to political forces even though they are not particularly interested in, or informed about, politics. Were they highly interested, they would be less flexible.

These arguments lead to a reassuring view of the American electorate. There is a widespread political stability based on a relatively stable social system. Political flexibility and sensitivity are provided by groups in between the partisans and therefore politically moderate groups. As long as the stable partisan groups are roughly of the same size, stable competitive conditions are guaranteed. As long as there is some overlapping of social groups, these will be the necessary cross pressures to produce the switching political moderates. It appears to be an electoral system with no weaknesses.

Nevertheless, there are some difficulties with this picture of an electoral system. For one thing, *the social cross pressure thesis is merely a tendency and not perfectly descriptive of the impact of social forces on political behavior.* The politically stable are more heterogeneous than the above account implies, and *the politically flexible are not under dramatic social cross pressure, according to the best data available.*

Discussion supporting the cross pressure thesis is most extensive in the Elmira study, *Voting,* by B. Berelson, P. Lazarsfeld, and W. McPhee. They found that the impact of cross pressure affects the time of individual decisions on how to vote. There was a slight tendency for cross pressures caused by religion and socioeconomic status to be associated with late decisions on voting. There were stronger relationships associated with conflicts in primary groups.

There is a stronger cross pressure relationship reported in *The American Voter,* although it predicts a somewhat different pattern behavior from those discussed above. The authors of *The American Voter* postulated that social cross pressures would lead to conflicting political attitudes. Table 3.6 shows the higher level of conflicting political attitudes among white-collar Catholics, the group under cross pressure presumably, in comparison with blue-collar Catholics for each number of attitudes.

TABLE 3.6
Proportion of Catholics Showing Some Conflict of Partisan Attitude by Occupation and Level of Attitude, 1956 (Survey Research Center, University of Michigan)

	Two Partisan Attitudes	Three Partisan Attitudes	Four Partisan Attitudes	Five Partisan Attitudes
Blue-collar	15%	45%	45%	74%
Business or professional	50%	47%	59%	85%

Source: Angus Campbell et al., *The American Voter* (New York: John Wiley and Sons, 1960), p. 88, Table 4.6.

Several other patterns of social variables have been treated as a source of cross pressure. One of these is upward and downward social mobility. To put it simply, the argument has been that upwardly mobile individuals abandon a Democratic identification and become Republicans, while the downwardly mobile abandon the Republican Party to become Democrats. During the period of maximum social and political stress associated with this mobility, the individual becomes an independent. It would be easier to test this argument if it were easier to measure social mobility. Table 3.7 from *The American Voter* uses change from first job to present job as a measure of occupational mobility, but the distributions in Table 3.7 do not provide much support for the hypothesis. There is, in fact, very little political difference between the upwardly and downwardly mobile, and this appears to hold for several measures of mobility.

TABLE 3.7

Relation of Reported Changes in Own Occupational Status to Changes in Self-Identification with Parties, 1956 (Survey Research Center, University of Michigan)

	OCCUPATIONAL MOBILITY	
	Down	Up
Changes in party identification		
From Republican to Democratic	28%	24%
From Republican to independent	8	12
From Democratic to independent	32	29
From Democratic to Republican	32	35
Total	100%	100%
n =	47	121

Source: Angus Campbell et al., *The American Voter* (New York: John Wiley and Sons, 1960), p. 459, Table 16.8.

Actually the only form of cross pressure that is strongly confirmed by national survey data is attitudinal cross pressure. When attitudes toward the candidates and parties were measured by the Survey Research Center in 1952 and 1956, conflicting attitudes—i.e., an individual holding pro-Democratic and pro-Republican attitudes—were associated with non-voting, indecision, and indifference toward the election. It is still not possible, however, to treat the conflicting attitudes as the cause of these patterns of behavior. It is quite possible that the attitudes and the withdrawal behavior is caused by some third factor.

The American electoral system appears to operate in a way predicted by the cross pressure hypothesis. There is partisan stability among both Republicans and Democrats, and the shifting of political fortunes is accomplished without intensity or extreme political appeals. We should, however, be skeptical of explaining these political patterns as a result of the social forces postulated by the cross pressure thesis. Neither short-run partisan stability nor independent flexibility appears strongly associated with social group predispositions. Two conclusions can be drawn about social characteristics and voting behavior. On the one hand, social factors like race, religion, and occupation, as well as primary groups, have been shown to be related to partisanship. *The long-run social and political patterns in the American electorate appear related.* On the other hand, the short-run impact of social groups on voting behavior appears uneven and insignificant generally. Occasionally social groups appear important nationally, as religion did in 1960, and under certain conditions social cross pressures may operate; but *normally we do not expect social factors to show the same consistent, strong patterns with vote choice that we have found with partisanship.*

4

Public Opinion and Ideology

Voting behavior is not the only significant aspect of American political behavior. Several aspects of the study of public opinion are not directly related to voting behavior. One persistent concern of analysis of public opinion is the attitudes of people toward issues of the day. Another concern is political ideology, particularly liberalism-conservatism and internationalism-isolationism, and of increasing interest is consensus, or the beliefs of the general public about how the political system should work.

PUBLIC OPINION ON POLITICAL ISSUES

The commercial opinion polling organizations have spent thirty years asking Americans about their views on matters of public policy. Most of this investigation has taken the form of asking individuals whether they "approve or disapprove of," "agree or disagree" with a statement of policy or of asking them to pick their preference among two or more alternative statements of policy. This form of questioning seriously exaggerates the number of people who hold views on political issues. People can easily say "agree" or "disapprove" in response to a question even if they know nothing at all about the topic. If given the opportunity, many people will volunteer the information that they hold no views on the matters of public policy. As recently as 1964 over one-third of the American electorate had no opinion on U.S. involvement in Vietnam. Table 4.1 from *The American Voter* shows the proportion of the electorate admitting that it had no opinions on major policy questions in 1956. The proportion with no opinion on an issue varies from one-tenth to almost one-third of the electorate, and to these proportions may be added as substantially uninformed those individuals who hold an opinion but who do not have any idea what the government is doing in the policy area. Beyond these two categories of relatively uninformed individuals, the work of Philip Converse shows that among the individuals who appear to have an opinion there are a number who ought to be regarded as responding to policy questions at random.[1]

There are a number of ways of explaining this lack of opinion and information on topics of public policy. Generally the same factors which explain non-voting account for the absence of opinions. *Individuals with little interest in, or concern with, politics are least likely to have opinions on matters of public policy.* Beyond this basic relationship low socioeconomic status is associated with no opinion on issues; *low income and little education create social circumstances in which individuals are less likely to have views and information on public policies.*

FUNCTIONS OF OPINIONS FOR INDIVIDUALS

Most discussions of political opinions imply a more or less reasoned handling of opinions by individuals; that is, that individuals intelligently relate their opinions to one another and that there is a logical relation between goals and preferences for policies leading to goals. While undoubtedly there is much reasoned opinion formation in the American public, not all opinions are mere rational deductions from goals and means to those goals. Social psychology suggests that an individual's opinions can serve various purposes: cognitive, social, and psychological. This consideration raises the possibility that opinions may not be related to political behavior and that political opinions may not be related to one another.

[1] Philip Converse, "The Nature of Belief Systems in Mass Publics," in David Apter, ed., *Ideology and Discontent* (New York: The Free Press of Glencoe, 1964), pp. 238-45.

TABLE 4.1
Public Familiarity with Selected Issues, 1956 (Survey Research Center, University of Michigan)

ISSUE	NO OPINION	HOLD OPINION BUT DO NOT KNOW WHAT GOV'T IS DOING	HOLD OPINION, KNOW WHAT GOV'T IS DOING	TOTAL
Foreign Policy				
Give aid to neutral countries	28%	19	53	100%
Send soldiers abroad	20%	13	67	100%
Economic aid to foreign countries	17%	16	67	100%
Act tough toward Russia, China	20%	11	69	100%
Avoid foreign involvement	14%	15	71	100%
Friendliness toward other nations	12%	10	78	100%
Domestic Policy				
Firing of suspected Communists	16%	39	45	100%
Leave electricity, housing to private industry	30%	19	51	100%
Segregation of schools	12%	34	54	100%
Influence of big business in government	23%	18	54	100%
Influence of unions in government	25%	20	55	100%
Insure medical care	12%	29	59	100%
Cutting taxes	19%	18	63	100%
Government guarantee of jobs	10%	23	67	100%
Racial equality in jobs and housing	14%	19	67	100%
Government aid to education	10%	23	67	100%

Source: Angus Campbell et al., *The American Voter* (New York: John Wiley and Sons, 1960), p. 174, Table 4-1.

To put it very simply, an opinion may serve purposes for an individual that are not dependent on its social, economic, or political meaning but rather depend on elements of the opinion's having special psychological significance for an individual. For example, an individual might hold opinions strongly prejudicial against some group because it enhances his self-esteem to feel superior to some others, or he might imagine that some group has undesirable qualities of which he rids himself by projecting them onto the group. An individual may view a political situation, say the clash between the United States and China, as analogous to more personal conflict situations to which he attaches considerable emotion. There are no limits to the possible attachments of psychological significance to elements of public opinion, but the importance of these attachments should not be exaggerated. The danger or disadvantage of psychological attachments of this kind is that the opinions are not responsive to ordinary influence because of their psychological importance to the individual. Either because of widespread personality characteristics or because of the low salience of political issues, *most Americans do not appear to attach strong psychological meaning to their political opinions* or at least not such strong emotional associations that political opinions are highly inflexible. Furthermore *it is unlikely in a modern pluralistic society that an opinion on a significant political subject will remain solely of psychological relevance for an individual; the opinion will also take on social and cognitive functions.*

Opinions serve a social function if they aid the individual in adjusting to others or in becoming part of a group. In some cases individuals may use opinions to set themselves apart from others. Political and social issues may be too unimportant generally to serve social purposes for most people, and there is little evidence to indicate that there are strong social conformity pressures on most political issues. Nevertheless for highly salient issues it is likely to be uncomfortable and costly for an individual to hold a socially unacceptable view. Cognitive functions of opinions cover the efforts to give meaning to our social environment and to relate elements of belief and meaning to one another. Generally opinions relate directly or indirectly to an individual's most salient goals or values; somehow the policy supported by a political opinion is expected to be consistent with one's most important political values. This is not necessarily the case, as sometimes an individual's opinions are inconsistent.

OPINION CONSISTENCY AND DISSONANCE

The main thrust of scholarly interest in the functions of opinions has been in analysis of opinion change. The general conclusion can be stated simply: *in order to change an opinion its function (or functions) for the individual must be undermined or altered;* or, to put it somewhat differently, giving an individual more information or altering the policy implications of an opinion will not necessarily lead to opinion change. The individual may hold his views for the social or psychological purpose it serves, in which case to change the opinion one must undermine or alter the social or psychological purpose served by the views. Nevertheless I would still maintain the perspective on American public opinion which suggests that political opinions are most often changed simply by providing individuals with more information. This additional information may be no more than indications that many political leaders whom an individual respects hold a particular view or some new facts about the environment. The low salience of most political issues, plus the widespread emphasis on debate and discussion, leads to circumstances which improve the opportunities for changing opinions with information.

The analysis of inconsistency in opinions has much in common with the cross pressure thesis considered in chapter 3. This analysis of opinions in psychology has taken the form of identifying elements of several opinions as consistent with one another or as being in conflict (dissonant). Also it is assumed that dissonance is disturbing and that an individual will try to avoid or to reduce dissonance. Dissonant elements of opinion and information are ideas in conflict. Some examples of dissonance analysis should clarify these concepts.

If an individual believes that it is extremely undesirable to use atomic bombs under any circumstances and also believes that the United States must do whatever is necessary to halt communism in Southeast Asia, these two opinions are potentially dissonant. Yet an individual might avoid holding strongly dissonant opinions such as "The United States should use atomic bombs in Southeast Asia in order to stop communism," or "The United States must not take certain steps in opposing communism." Or he may avoid dissonance by holding the view that it would be unwise to use atomic bombs in Southeast Asia since the communists would turn it to their advantage, or some other opinion that reconciles the potential conflict in the original opinions.

If an individual believes that it is appropriate to treat blacks as an inferior because he believes they are of inferior intelligence and ability and if he is confronted with new information that blacks are equal to whites in intelligence and ability, these two elements are in conflict. The dissonance could be reduced by discrediting the source of the new information or by rationalizing his attitude toward blacks on some other basis such as moral or spiritual superiority of whites.

Cognitively consistent patterns are presumably stable, while dissonant patterns are susceptible to change. Furthermore individuals supposedly will change dissonant patterns in the easiest way; the opinions or beliefs that are least important to the individual will be changed rather than the salient, important ideas or values.

AGGREGATE OPINIONS

It is no simple matter to describe the distributions of opinions in the American electorate because there is no obvious, agreed way in which to measure these opinions. Or, to put it another way, by asking different questions in public opinion polls we can get different answers. We could substantially alter distributions of opinions on, say, foreign aid by asking respondents if they approved of "squandering our money abroad" as opposed to "feeding starving children overseas." Furthermore, there is no ultimate test of measures of opinions as there is with voting behavior. Consequently descriptions of public opinion must be taken as more subjective, more tentative than the discussion of partisanship because there are no independent indicators of opinions on public issues.

Usually public attitudes on policies in American society are viewed as *permissive opinion,* that is, there is a wide range of government activity acceptable to the public, and ordinarily policy alternatives advocated by the political parties are within the range of permissive agreement. *Negative opinion* exists to the extent there are alternatives which are definitely opposed by the public, and *supportive opinion* exists to the extent that certain policies are demanded. For example, there is undoubtedly widespread supportive opinion for public education in this country; most individuals demand a system of public education or would demand it if it were threatened. At the same time there is permissive support for a wide range of policies and programs in public education. Governments at several levels may engage in a variety of programs without the public's becoming aroused to opposition or support. Within this permissive range the public is indifferent. At some point out-and-out opposition to programs in public education develops, and negative opinion is formed which imposes a limit on how far government can go. It is no easy matter for political analysts or politicians to discover these boundaries between supportive, permissive, and negative opinions, and political leaders deceptively or mistakenly argue that there are supportive opinions for their positions and negative opinions toward their opponents' views. We should be skeptical of these claims because it is much more likely that there are permissive opinions and casual indifferences toward the alternative views. Even when individuals express preferences on public policies, these are not likely to be deeply felt and probably represent permissive opinion.

ATTITUDES TOWARD PUBLIC POLICY

There are three common divisions of American opinion on public policy: domestic economic affairs, other domestic affairs, and foreign affairs, in addition to the more general areas of ideology and consensus. The following analysis will investigate each of the areas separately, their interrelationships, and the relationship of social characteristics and partisanship with opinions on issues. The leading assumption is that partisan identification provides guidance for the public on policy matters; that is, most Americans hold their opinions by following what they perceive to be the view consistent with their partisanship.

One of the basic beliefs of American politics has been that economic issues are more salient, have more impact on the electorate than other issues. Domestic economic issues are frequently treated by politicians and political analysts as the real forces at work in the political system, sometimes openly and sometimes behind a facade of other issues. There is a certain plausibility to this view—obviously there have been periods when economic issues were paramount—but there is no reason to assume that any one type of issue will always be more important than others. Doubtless there is variation in the salience of issues, with economic issues frequently the most prominent and occasionally displaced by foreign policy issues or non-economic domestic issues. In any case in recent years it appears that for some members of the electorate issues like school integration or a Catholic in the White House or escalation of the war in Vietnam have been of far greater concern than economic issues. And by 1968 in national politics economic issues had taken a secondary role in comparison with Vietnam, law and order, and integration.

It is not easy to establish the relative salience of domestic affairs and foreign affairs; moreover, the measures of salience are quite crude. V. O. Key reports in *Public Opinion and American Democracy*[2] that in discussing the merits and demerits of the parties and candidates in 1952 and 1956 Americans gave domestic matters greater salience than foreign affairs. The breakdown he gives is as follows:

	1952	1956
Foreign affairs more salient	16%	17%
Domestic affairs more salient	47	54
About equal attention to each	8	10
No issue content	29	19

V. O. Key also reports that there was a clear relationship between issue salience and voting, with those who gave greater or equal salience to foreign affairs voting for Eisenhower disproportionately. This is merely descriptive of what has happened in recent elections and according to only one form of measurement; that is,

[2] V. O. Key, Jr., *Public Opinion and American Democracy* (New York: Alfred A. Knopf, 1961), p. 173.

it is simply one way of describing an extremely complex set of factors and interrelationships. Although economic issues are likely always to be important in politics, the central role of economic issues can no longer be taken for granted.

DOMESTIC ECONOMIC ISSUES

In economic matters Americans are more liberal than conservative. The overall configuration of preferences on public policy in the American electorate can be described as "liberal" in that there is usually a willingness to support federal governmental programs intended to solve social problems. There is no widespread, consistent public opposition to increased government activity in domestic economic affairs and in welfare programs. In recent years the main source of opposition to federal government activities appears to be based on opposition to racial integration and not based on economic considerations. To be sure, there are individuals in the electorate who oppose government economic activities for other reasons, but the ideological opponents of government activity are not numerous in the general public. In this respect, as in many others, the public does not reflect the characteristics of the political leaders among whom there are many opponents of "liberal" domestic economic programs. In this respect political leaders are much more conservative than the public.

Figure 4.1 shows some distributions of political attitudes taken from Survey Research Center national samples. Only the 1956 and 1960 questions are perfectly comparable, so it is not possible to assess accurately changes in public opinion from 1956 to 1968 with these data. There is considerable stability in the aggregate level of support for federal aid to education and medical care programs over the twelve-year period. Generally over 50 percent of the electorate favors these programs with about one-quarter of the population in opposition and the remainder holding qualified views. In recent years there has been a decline in support for federal aid to education.

It is certainly reasonable to expect that views on such issues would be strongly influenced by an individual's social and economic characteristics. Figure 4.2 shows the level of support for

FIGURE 4.1

The Support for Federal Aid to Education, Medical Care for the Aged, and School Integration from 1956 to 1968

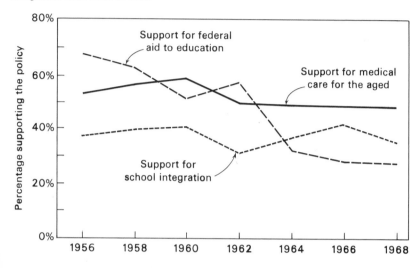

Source: Survey Research Center, University of Michigan.

medical care in various social groupings in 1964 and 1968. The highest level of support is found among blacks and Jews, traditionally liberal groups; and while these groups are similar politically, they are extremely dissimilar socially and economically. The blacks, a low-income group, could be expected to need government assistance to secure medical care; immediate self-interest could explain their support, as it could explain the support of retired people. But the Jews are a white-collar, high-income group and most unlikely to hold these views for reasons of self-interest. The Jewish group, more than any of those considered here, represents the impact of ideology and social doctrine on political opinions. In the other groups there is a gradual increase of support as we move from the white-collar occupations through manual laborers to the farmers and retired. In general, there is considerable stability in attitudes between the two years.

It should be noted that partisans have quite different views on medical care. Democratic partisans support medical care strongly, and Republican partisans oppose medical care to about

FIGURE 4.2
Support for Medical Care for the Aged in 1964 and 1968 according to Region, Race, Religion, and Occupation

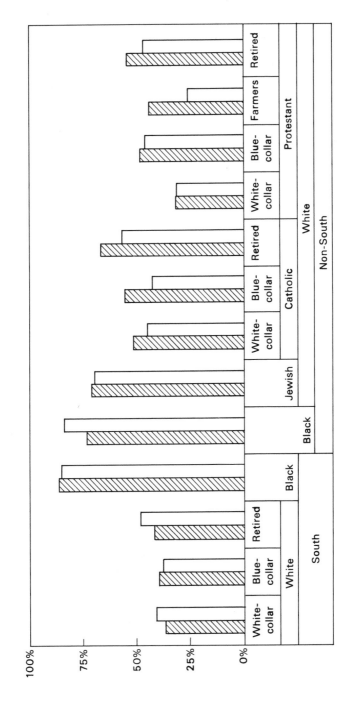

Source: Survey Research Center, University of Michigan.

83

the same degree. Partisanship may not lead individuals to hold the views they do, but the stability of an individual's partisanship makes it likely that his views on policy are influences by his partisanship. Individuals abandon their party over an issue presumably only when they have exceptionally intense feelings about the issue. It should be noted that there are extreme or intense differences on very few issues among social groups or among partisans. Seemingly neither social circumstances nor political parties provides such unambiguously persuasive cues for most individuals that their own values and misperceptions cannot operate independently. Political, social, and personal factors all diminish the dramatic differences that might exist on public issues.

CIVIL RIGHTS AND INTEGRATION

The main topics of domestic policy on non-economic matters since World War II have dealt with civil liberties, racial integration, and law and order issues. In the early 1950s a cluster of issues and problems, loosely covered by the term *McCarthyism*, was raised over the rights and treatment of individuals accused of treason, socialistic attitudes, and various other acts and beliefs. The general public was never as concerned with McCarthyism as the politically attentive were. In the electorate, concern with McCarthyism—either pro or con—never became an element of significant division among social or political groups.

The most persistently volatile issues in American history have dealt with problems surrounding the treatment of blacks. After many years of little public attention to these problems, integration in the form of the courts' desegregation of Southern schools became a major focus of national and international attention. Two significant developments in the distribution of attitudes are associated with this issue. First, over the past fifteen years Southern blacks had become increasingly concerned with public policies affecting them and had changed from a largely apathetic, uninterested group to a concerned, involved, politically motivated group. Second, large numbers of Southern whites adjusted their opinions to accept the realities of the new legal and political position of blacks. White Southerners did not come to prefer integrated schools, but many became willing to accept them.

Figure 4.1 shows a consistency over eight years in support for, and opposition to, school integration in the adult population, and Figure 4.3 shows how unevenly this support is distributed among social groups in 1964 and 1968. Support for school integration is high among blacks both in the South and North, and support is low among Southern whites. Among Northern whites the more dramatic differences are associated with religious preference, while relatively minor variation is associated with occupational groupings except for farmers, who display consistently lower levels of support for integrated schools.

There are differences in support for school integration associated with partisanship, although when blacks are eliminated from the distributions the differences among partisans are not as great as the differences found among social groups. In the North, even though Democrat partisans support integration most frequently and Republican partisans least frequently among independents and weak partisans, the pattern is uneven. In the South among whites, support for integration has varied among partisan groupings, but there is no consistent pattern. On the integration issue, in contrast to the domestic economic issues, the distributions of partisanship do not explain the differences. Probably issues like integration are regularly more related to social groups than to political categories. In part this may be because the leaders of both parties take similar stands on such issues in a given constituency; consequently the parties do not provide differing cues or leadership. In other cases the leaders of one party may disagree among themselves on such issues, perhaps because the leaders represent differing constituencies, and consequently a party will not offer consistent cues and leadership on these matters of public policy. In some circumstances these issues have sufficient salience to overcome the influence of partisan political leadership.

Another area of domestic policy that has received attention is the relation of governmental institutions to religious organizations and particularly state support for parochial education and prayers in public schools. As with the other areas of non-economic domestic policy, in part the public is responding to Supreme Court decisions. Attitudes toward parochial school support are heavily influenced by an individual's perceived religious interests. Generally Americans would prefer more mixing of church and state, not

FIGURE 4.3
Support for School Integration according to Region, Race, Religion, and Occupation in 1964 and 1968

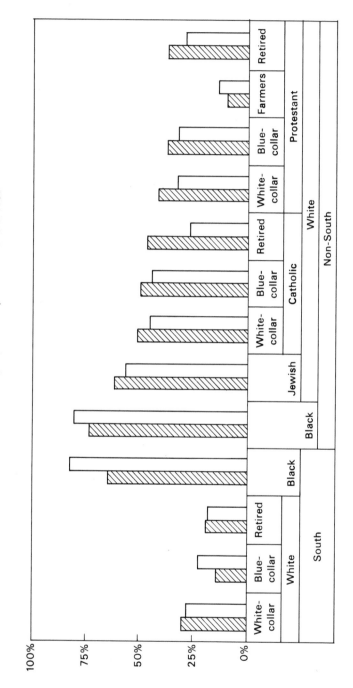

Source: Survey Research Center, University of Michigan.

less. For example, about three-fourths of adults support the practice of starting public school classes with a prayer. But to date this preference has not been mobilized into an intense preference or into a political force of any consequence nationally. Issues which might have become volatile politically have been suppressed by the leaders of major religious institutions among others, but the area remains as a temptation to political leaders searching for subjects on which to take potentially popular stands.

In the late 1960s a cluster of issues under the general topic of "law and order" became salient and subsequently played a prominent role in national and local elections. The 1968 Survey Research Center study asked respondents whether they thought the solution to the problems of rioting, law, and order was through tougher enforcement or through removing causes like poverty. About one-fourth of the electorate supported tougher law enforcement as the way to restore order, and about one-third supported removing the causes of trouble. Figure 4.4 shows these views were rather unevenly distributed in various social groupings. Perhaps the most dramatic differences are between blacks, who reveal little inclination to support tougher law enforcement as a cure for disorder, and whites, who are much more likely to support tougher law enforcement and unlikely to support removing poverty as a cause of disorder. The Jewish members of the electorate occupy a middle position, and with this exception neither religion nor occupation discriminates on the issue among whites. There is a slight tendency for young people to support tougher law enforcement more strongly than older people do; this tendency is reflected in the attitudes among retired people in Figure 4.4.

There is no relationship among partisan categories that cannot be completely accounted for by the disproportionate concentration of blacks among Democrats. In other words, once we control for race there is no tendency for either view of law and order to be related to Democratic or Republican leanings.

FOREIGN AFFAIRS

Like non-economic domestic problems, foreign affairs vary greatly in salience and particularly in response to involvement of the

FIGURE 4.4
Support for Law and Order in 1968 according to Region, Race, Religion, and Occupation

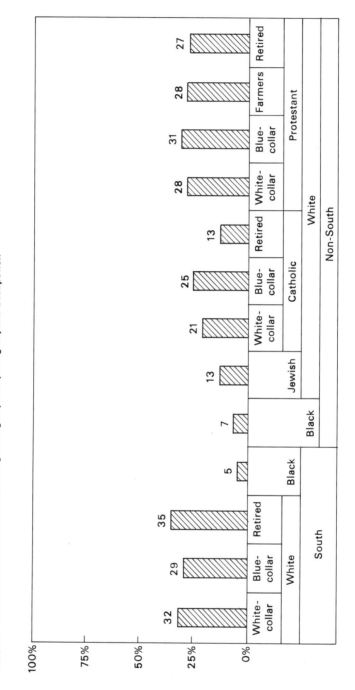

Source: Survey Research Center, University of Michigan.

nation in military conflicts. In recent years the main issue of foreign policy has become concern over military policies in Vietnam. In 1964 the alleged "trigger-happy" approach of Goldwater to international problems became an issue for large numbers of voters and was emphasized by Democrats. Whether justified or not, Goldwater's appeal suffered because he was viewed as recklessly belligerent and more likely than his opponent to involve the country in military conflicts. This served as a curtain-raiser for the growing salience of Vietnam leading up to the election of 1968.

In the Johnson-Goldwater race Vietnam was not yet the overwhelming issue that it had become by 1968. In 1964 over one-third of the electorate had no opinion on questions about Vietnam, but by 1968 the proportion was reduced to only one in ten with no opinion. As an issue of public policy, U.S. involvement in Vietnam has fascinating characteristics. Perhaps the most significant feature of public opinion in this regard is the slow pace of awareness of the seriousness of U.S. involvement and the slow increase of disenchantment and criticism with the course of the Vietnam war. The general public was much slower than opinion elites to respond to the issue. Figure 4.5 shows the patterns of responses for several questions about Vietnam asked of Survey Research Center national samples in 1964, 1966, and 1968 with the addition of response to two questions asked in 1970 by the Gallup Poll. These responses are based on a question about whether we did the right thing in getting involved in Vietnam or whether we should have stayed out. The second question asked was whether we should pull out or take a stronger stand in Vietnam. Large proportions of respondents, usually about one-third, preferred the present situation to either alternative.

The overall tendency is clear: an increasingly widespread belief that we should have stayed out of Vietnam. To a slight degree Republicans are more likely to hold this view than Democrats. This configuration should not be interpreted as especially "dovish," since some people believe it was a mistake to get involved but believe that once there, we should win at all costs. A better indication of hawk-dove sentiment is given by the responses to a second question, which asked whether the U.S. should pull out immediately or take a stronger stand even if it means invading North Vietnam. Support for a stronger stand has

FIGURE 4.5

Attitudes toward U.S. Involvement in Vietnam, 1964 to 1970

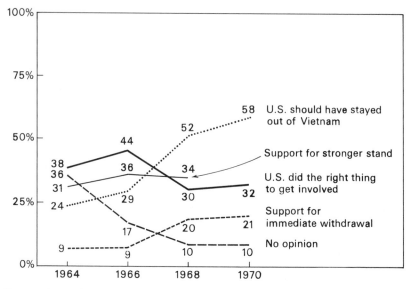

Sources: Survey Research Center, University of Michigan; and Gallup Poll.

aThis question was not strictly comparable to the earlier questions. *The Gallup Opinion Index* (Princeton, N.J.: Gallup International, Inc., 1970), Report No. 56, February, 1970, p. 2.

remained stable since 1964 with about one-third of the electorate favoring an escalation of the war. In earlier years popular support for prompt withdrawal was low, less than 10 percent, but by 1968 had increased to 20 percent. In popular jargon the issue has become more polarized as it has become more salient.

Figure 4.6 shows the social location in 1968 of attitudes supporting withdrawal and a stronger stand. Several social characteristics are associated with support for immediate withdrawal from Vietnam and generally the pattern is that retired people, Jews, and blacks approve withdrawal, while the remaining groups, regardless of occupation, religion, or region, show consistently lower levels of support for withdrawal. In general, the reverse relationship holds for taking a stronger stand in Vietnam except there is more variation in the proportions. For example, several groups in both the North and the South reveal well over 40 percent in favor of a stronger stand in Vietnam. Low levels of

FIGURE 4.6
Support for Immediate Withdrawal or a Stronger Stand in Vietnam in 1968 according to Region, Race, Religion, and Occupation

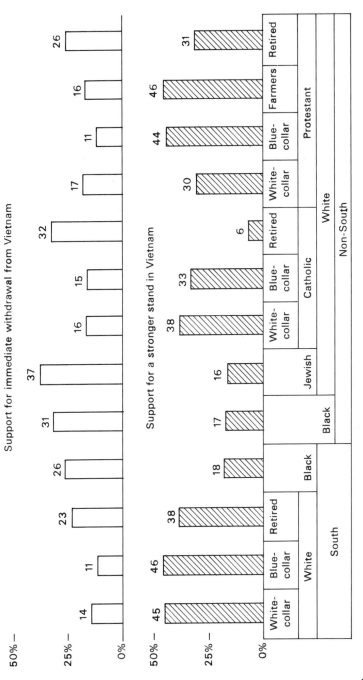

Support for immediate withdrawal from Vietnam

Support for a stronger stand in Vietnam

Source: Survey Research Center, University of Michigan.

91

support for a stronger stand are among blacks and Jews but inconsistently distributed among the retired.

There are no differences between Democrats and Republicans on these attitudes, but there is a tendency for independents to be more hawkish than either Democrats or Republicans. This relationship holds in all regions of the country.

Since so much attention has been given the young people who are intensely opposed to the war in Vietnam, the findings in Figure 4.7 may be surprising. There is a fairly consistent tendency for Americans to be more hawkish the younger they are. If there is

FIGURE 4.7
The Distribution of Attitudes Supporting Stronger Stand in Vietnam according to Age, 1968

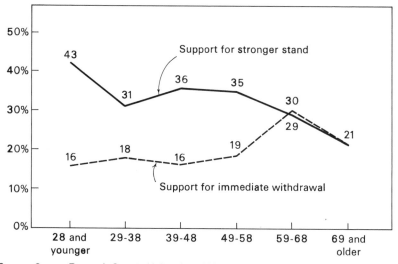

Source: Survey Research Center, University of Michigan.

anything resembling a generation gap, it does not run in the expected direction on the Vietnam issue. There is not even a dramatic division of opinion within the younger age cohorts; the greatest polarization on the Vietnam issue occurs within the older age groupings. College students are a minority of their age group, but according to surveys by the Gallup Poll even college students were hawkish prior to 1968; only since 1968 have college students become more in favor of immediate withdrawal from Vietnam than has the general public.[3]

The polarization of opinion among young people emerges as we look at the Vietnam issue and attitudes toward school integration jointly distributed in Table 4.2. The circled proportions, representing liberal on both issues or conservative on both, show that larger proportions of the youngest group are either liberal on both or conservative on both. The differences are not great, however, and the comparisons here do not entail the

TABLE 4.2
Attitudes toward Vietnam and School Integration according to Age, 1968

	Does Not Support Stronger Stand in Vietnam	Supports Stronger Stand in Vietnam	
Favors school integration	(28)	11	under 28 years old
Does not favor school integration	20	(31) /100% n = 249	
	(25)	11	29 to 59 years old
	31	(22) /100% n = 891	
	(17)	6	over 59 years old
	38	(17) /100% n = 392	

Source: Survey Research Center, University of Michigan.

[3] *The Gallup Opinion Index* (Princeton, N.J.: Gallup International, Inc., 1970), Report No. 55, January, 1970, p. 16.

intensity or the extremes of opinion that polarization often implies. Nonetheless, differences within age cohorts appear more dramatic in several comparisons than do the differences across age cohorts. The conservatism of the youngest age group will be discussed again in chapter 5, as they are discovered to have been a disproportionately strong source of Wallace votes in 1968.

Generally partisanship is strongly related to domestic economic policies, and partisan loyalties appear to dominate the attitudes that individuals have which might be associated with social and economic groupings independently of political party ties. *Opinions on foreign policy, by way of contrast, are not related to party identification,* and the moderate relationships are with social and economic characteristics. *Attitudes toward various race issues seem related to both partisanship and social variables, with the latter the more important.* The sustained investigation of attitudes toward public policies is made difficult by the relatively short time any particular issue is salient and by the changing position of the political parties over the years. In addition, a given issue may strike social groups differently over time. With so many elements of change in attitudes toward public policy, it is difficult to isolate the various sources of influence.

LIBERALISM-CONSERVATISM

Most commentators on the American political scene—not to mention the active participants—describe much of what happens in terms of liberalism and conservatism. Political history (and current news analysis) is portrayed as "trends of liberalism," "middle-of-the-road policies," "rejection of conservatism." Analysts characterize candidates and political parties as liberal and conservative; within each party leaders and platforms are alleged to be relatively liberal and conservative. The major problem is to assess the importance of this variable in mass public opinion and, more specifically, to decide if individuals in society are self-consciously oriented to politics as liberals, middle-of-the-roaders, or conservatives, and to determine whether individuals use this ideological orientation to organize political information and attitudes. In other words, does political ideology play a role for Americans similar to the role of partisanship as a basic determinant of their specific political views?

Survey Research Center data reported in *The American Voter* show that very few members of the electorate discuss their evaluations of the parties and the candidates in ideological language, fewer than 15 percent in 1956.[4] The incidence of words like "liberal" and "conservative" in the voters' discussions of parties and candidates during an ideological campaign like 1964 was only a little greater than in a non-ideological campaign as 1956. *The overwhelming weight of evidence indicates that most voters do not evaluate candidates or select their political parties in conformity with an ideological commitment.*[5] As with other political ideas in the minds of Americans, political ideologies are vague, superficial labels applied rather indifferently in their environment.

On the other hand, when Americans are asked to identify themselves as liberals or conservatives, they are able to do so. The categories obviously have some meaning for most Americans; the categories simply are not of overriding importance. According to this uncomplicated measure of self-identification, the electorate has usually been assessed at about one-third middle-of-the-road, one-third liberal, and one-third conservative. There may be a tendency for Americans to think of themselves as more conservative in recent years, for a 1964 study by Free and Cantril finds that over 60 percent of all adults think of themselves as more conservative than their parents.[6]

It is also possible to draw on the study by Free and Cantril to investigate the relationship between ideological self-identification and partisan self-identification, Table 4.3 showing the distribution. The data array shows that liberals are disproportionately Democrat, Republicans are disproportionately conservative, and independents tend to be middle-of-the-roaders. But conservatives are about equally likely to be Democrats as Republicans, and Democrats are not much more likely to be liberal than conserva-

[4] Angus Campbell et al., *The American Voter,* p. 249.

[5] John C. Pierce, "Ideology, Attitudes, and Voting Behavior of the American Electorate: 1956, 1960, 1964" (Ph.D. diss., University of Minnesota, 1969), Table 3.1, p. 63.

[6] Lloyd A. Free and Hadley Cantril, *The Political Beliefs of Americans* (New York: Simon and Schuster, 1968), p. 139..

tive. The relationship between ideology and partisanship may be shown in the low coincidence of Republican and liberal identifications.

TABLE 4.3
The Distribution of Ideological Self-identification and Partisan Self-identification, 1964

	Republican	Independent	Democrat
Liberal	4	6	19
Middle of the Road	8	11	18
Conservative	14	7	13
			100%
			n = 2905

Source: These data were recalculated with discrepancies averaged from data in Lloyd A. Free and Hadley Cantril, *The Political Beliefs of Americans* (New York: Simon and Schuster, 1968), pp. 204, 205, 224, 235. The interviewing was done by the Gallup Poll.

Some analysts have attempted to create measures of liberalism-conservatism from answers to questions on public policy. Several general conclusions can be drawn from these efforts. First, in the national electorate there is not a strong, consistent ordering of individuals on a liberal-conservative dimension if a large number of specific public policies are used. Or, to put it differently, *Americans are not consistently liberal, conservative, or moderate on a wide range of issues.* A given individual will be liberal on farm issues, conservative on labor union issues, moderate on education, and so on. A second individual will be liberal on labor matters, moderate on education, and conservative on farm policy. When viewed collectively, these individuals' opinions form no single consistent pattern, even though each individual's attitudes might be reasonable enough for him. Since it is likely that many individual responses to questions of public policy have little meaning or salience for the individual, *the absence of a strong liberal-conservative dimension on issues reflects the unimportance of the issues for the electorate.*

As the range of issues narrows, the positions taken by the public show less variation and inconsistency. A fairly stable attitude dimension on welfare policies and government economic activity has been documented in *The American Voter.*[7] Although this domestic economic activity measure is related to party identification (Democrats are more liberal; Republicans are more conservative), *domestic economic issue positions are not related to attitudes on other domestic issues or attitudes toward foreign policy.* Table 4.4 from V. O. Key's *Public Opinion and American Democracy* shows the common pattern of no relationship between liberalism-conservatism and internationalism-isolationism. The two dimensions appear quite independent of one another in the general public, even though the dimensions may be interrelated among political leaders.

TABLE 4.4
Relation of Position on Domestic Liberalism Scale to Position on Internationalism Scale, 1956 (Survey Research Center, University of Michigan)

INTERNATIONALISM	LIBERALISM		
	Low	Medium	High
High	50%	59%	58%
Medium	32	28	21
Low	18	13	21
Total	100%	100%	100%
n =	226	598	491

Source: V. O. Key, Jr., *Public Opinion and American Democracy* (New York: Alfred A. Knopf, 1961), p. 158, Table 7.2.

Attitudes toward public policies are influenced by several factors:

1) Some individuals undoubtedly take stands on issues in order to be consistent with a general ideological position or to be consistent with a general commitment like opposition to federal government programs or support for military aid to non-communist countries.

2) Some individuals take a stand on an issue to be consistent with their political party or to agree with a political leader whom they support.

3) Some individuals favor or oppose a policy because they believe they have important interests at stake.

[7] Angus Campbell et al., *The American Voter,* pp. 194-97.

If everyone had a strong ideology, their attitudes would be determined by their ideology. To a considerable extent this appears to happen to the most politically alert and concerned in our society, but this group is only a very small minority of the total adult population. If our major political parties were ideologically oriented, then by following the parties or political leaders in our parties, Americans would have their opinions determined indirectly by ideology. But our two major political parties are notoriously non-ideological—many of the leaders have personal ideological commitments, but no single ideology dominates the parties. Finally neither ideology nor party loyalty is important enough for most people to determine their attitudes toward policy if they believe extremely important interests are at stake. In fact, most Americans ignore ideology and misperceive their party's position if they hold a strong view on a public policy, and if they discover that their party or ideology is in conflict with their interests, Americans weaken their support of their usual party or ideology.

Usually specific matters of public policy are of little interest to the electorate; as a consequence, the political parties are unconcerned with dramatizing particular policies. Under these circumstances most attitudes toward public policies are extremely casual views. It is relatively unusual in American politics for an issue to become so important that it disrupts party loyalties for large numbers of people. *But in the rare case when individuals feel important interests are at stake, it is most unlikely that party loyalty or ideological beliefs will overcome strongly felt interests.*

LIBERALISM AND CONSERVATISM AS PERSONALITY FACTORS

Due mainly to the work of Herbert McClosky the liberalism-conservatism dimension has been applied in political analysis in a way not directly related to public policy or political parties. In his "Conservatism and Personality,"[8] McClosky developed an index of liberalism-conservatism that measures personality or individual style. McClosky documented a wide array of relationships between

[8] Herbert McClosky, "Conservatism and Personality," *American Political Science Review,* Vol. 52 (March, 1958), 27-45.

psychological variables and liberalism-conservatism. His findings suggest that there are basic orientations toward governmental activity and the nature of society which could, under the right circumstances, influence political behavior. These personality measures of liberalism-conservatism are not associated with Democratic and Republican Party loyalty or voting behavior. Of course, there is no reason to expect personality factors to be associated with party loyalty or vote choice or public policy views, but this means that the applications of McClosky's work are somewhat limited to date.[9]

Two other major attempts to relate personality characteristics to political behavior should be mentioned. Extremist political beliefs and activities have been a central concern of social scientists even though in American society extremists are a tiny fraction of the whole society. Extremist groups draw members from all parts of society. In particular, right-wing extremists like the John Birch Society appear to have members of high social status; groups like the Ku Klux Klan and the Black Muslims have members of low social status. More important, individuals attracted to extremist groups are likely to have a cluster of atypical personality characteristics including anxiety, hostility, and insecurity. These generalizations must be considered highly tentative, since there are only a few studies of extremists in American society.[10]

A different approach to the study of ideology and personality has been launched by Robert Lane.[11] His efforts to show that individual political styles and beliefs are based on personality characteristics have been limited to a small number of cases; thus the results cannot be extended easily to the American public. Nevertheless, Lane demonstrates that many elements of ideological belief and political style have psychological roots.

---

[9] Survey Research Center data show that individuals who shift political parties are distributed in such a way that those who shift toward the Republican Party are more likely to be conservative; those who shift toward the Democratic Party are less likely to be conservative.

[10] The major study in recent years is Daniel Bell, *The Radical Right* (Garden City, N.Y.: Doubleday Anchor Books, 1964).

[11] Robert E. Lane, *Political Ideology* (New York: The Free Press, 1962).

CONSENSUS ON "RULES OF THE GAME"

One further element of public opinion to be considered is the nature of support in the American political system for fundamental principles of a democratic society. A widely held and perfectly plausible belief is that the American public supports free speech for all, free elections, civil rights, and other operating rules of a democratic society. At a highly abstract level this is true enough. American citizens ascribe to the basic rules of democracy overwhelmingly when this commitment is kept vague and abstract. As individuals are asked about more and more precise applications of democratic principles, agreement disappears. Specifically there is no widespread agreement in the American electorate on extending civil rights and liberties to individuals with unpopular political and social opinions.

Two important qualifications are in order. First, the electorate's responses are attitudes which may have little meaning for them and are not measures of their behavior or even measures of their attitudes under circumstances of great concern for democratic principles. Furthermore, while it is apparently true that large numbers of Americans do not support democratic rules for all citizens, it does not necessarily follow that these same large numbers would support the denial of civil rights and liberties when faced with that alternative. Nevertheless it is a remarkable failure of American political education and socialization that there is not more firm support for the specific applications of American democratic traditions.

The second important qualification of these findings applies to the political, social, and economic leaders in American society who consistently support these democratic principles more strongly than the general public does. Usually support among leaders is so high that it is possible to conclude that the leaders in society defend and maintain democratic procedures. The leaders' consensus on democratic rights and values makes the weakness of the general public less crucial. National studies by Stouffer[12] and McClosky[13] support the view that leaders are stronger than the

[12]Samuel Stouffer, *Communism, Conformity and Civil Liberties* (Garden City, N.Y.: Doubleday, 1955).

[13]Herbert McClosky, "Consensus and Ideology in American Politics," *American Political Science Review,* Vol. 58 (June, 1964), 361-82.

public in support of "rules of the game." Table 4.5 from McClosky's study shows the degree to which leaders support the "rules of the game" in comparison with the public. Political influentials—in this study delegates and alternates to the Democratic and Republican national conventions in 1956—are consistently more likely to agree with "rules of the game" than is a sample of the electorate. It may not be reassuring to discover that 6.8 percent of the political influentials agree that "the majority has the right to abolish minorities if it wants to" or that 13.3 percent agree that "almost any unfairness or brutality may have to be justified when some great purpose is being carried out." But in both examples substantially greater proportions, one-quarter and one-third respectively, of the general electorate support these views. Presumably leaders are recruited and educated in such a way that they come prepared with, or develop agreement on, democratic procedures. Apparently leaders make decisions in society in a number of ways which maintain democratic practices even without widespread public support.

The widespread interest in public opinion and "rules of the game" has been based partly on two somewhat mistaken impressions. First, the popular concern with public attitudes on policy issues is based partially on the assumption that the public influences the making of policy, but actually we now believe that the public has little influence on policy formation and on most matters public opinion follows policy-making. The study of public opinion has not proved to be a significant aspect of policy-making studies. Second, there has been an assumption that stable democratic political systems rest on a nearly universal commitment to fundamental principles and their application, but the evidence on this point is inconclusive. Certainly a democratic system cannot long survive widespread, intense hostility, but probably the positive belief in particular operating procedures among the public is unnecessary. Hostility to democratic procedures is fatal, whether among the leaders or the public, but support of these procedures may prove essential only among leaders. Perhaps the public need not agree on basic principles so long as it does not demand disruptive policies and procedures.

In a different perspective the failure of public opinion to be as important as expected in these respects is a failure of the American political system to conform to simple democratic ideals

TABLE 4.5

Political Influentials vs. the Electorate: Response to Items Expressing "Rules of the Game"*

Items	Political Influentials	General Electorate
There are times when it almost seems better for the people to take the law into their own hands rather than wait for the machinery of government to act.	13.3%	26.9%
The majority has the right to abolish minorities if it wants to.	6.8%	28.4%
We might as well make up our minds that in order to make the world better a lot of innocent people will have to suffer.	27.2%	41.6%
If Congressional committees stuck strictly to the rules and gave every witness his rights, they would never succeed in exposing the many dangerous subversives they have turned up.	24.7%	47.4%
I don't mind a politician's methods if he manages to get the right things done.	25.6%	42.4%
Almost any unfairness or brutality may have to be justified when some great purpose is being carried out.	13.3%	32.8%
Politicians have to cut a few corners if they are going to get anywhere.	29.4%	43.2%
People ought to be allowed to vote even if they can't do so intelligently.	65.6%	47.6%
To bring about great changes for the benefit of mankind often requires cruelty and even ruthlessness.	19.4%	31.3%
Very few politicians have clean records, so why get excited about the mud-slinging that sometimes goes on?	14.8%	38.1%
It is all right to get around the law if you don't actually break it.	21.2%	30.2%
The true American way of life is disappearing so fast that we may have to use force to save it.	12.8%	34.6%
n =	3020	1484

Source: Herbert McClosky, "Consensus and Ideology in American Politics," in Edward Dreyer and Walter Rosenbaum, eds., *Public Opinion and Electoral Behavior* (Belmont, Calif.: Wadsworth Publishing Co., 1966), p. 243, Table I.

*Since respondents were forced to make a choice on each item, the number of omitted or "don't know" responses was, on the average, fewer than one percent, and thus has little influence on the direction or magnitude of the results reported in this table.

as developed in political theory. Democratic theory has given public opinion a prominent role, more prominent than found in reality. But this portrayal is not so much a dissent from democratic theory as it is a realization that democratic theory has focused on negative and supportive opinions, those rare circumstances in which the public demands a policy. But, in fact, policy disputes are almost always over matters of indifference to the public, the realm of permissive opinion. These findings follow from the basic indifference of Americans to politics and public policies and represent an abandonment of the role assigned the public in democratic theory, a role calling for considerably greater interest, information, and vigilance. But in truth the high degree of concern postulated for the public in democratic theory may only accompany social and political crises of such intensity that democracy itself is in jeopardy. It has been argued that the political indifference of Americans is a sign of social and economic health.

This conclusion would be more comforting if it were not suspected that these configurations of opinion were a basic weakness in our political system. Specifically the public provides support for the political leaders, but the ignorance and apathy in leaders' followings is a potential weakness. A leader's following is vulnerable to irrelevant and inappropriate appeals. The failure of the following to understand policy and "rules of the game" means that they cannot be counted on to support the leader on the basis of policies or principles. Under the worst circumstances democratic leaders might lose support to undemocratic leaders without the followers' realizing what was happening. Less dramatically, and doubtless more commonly, leaders who support policies beneficial to their following lose support to leaders whose policies are inappropriate for the following on the basis of some irrelevent and insignificant issue.

The last chapter considers the role of issues in support of candidates in elections—the most likely form of influence by the public over policy.

5

Campaigns and Electoral Decisions

Most Americans become sufficiently concerned with Presidential elections and even state and local elections to be interested in finding out who wins and to pay attention to highlights of the campaigns. Undeniably American political campaigns are an extraordinary set of practices. For all the foolishness and viciousness occasionally present during a campaign, elections are an important method of arousing public interest in politics and issues and a most important technique for selecting and rejecting political leaders. Political campaigns have several purposes.

1) to increase turnout for candidates or a referendum;

2) to publicize the attractive qualities of candidates, platforms and performance; and

3) to raise money and to recruit workers for the campaign. The payoff for these efforts is victory on election day. It is desirable to assess the nature and impact of campaign activities.

CAMPAIGN PARTICIPATION

The greatest spectacle of American politics, the Presidential campaign and election, involves about four million workers in telephoning, doorbell ringing, addressing envelopes, and doing the work of the campaign. While this is a large number, it is fewer people than participate annually in amateur theatricals or engage in almost any other kind of volunteer activity. A rather small proportion of American citizens is attracted to campaign work, considering the crucial role of elections in our political system. As Table 5.1 shows, there was a slight increase in campaign workers during the period from 1952 to 1968. While there is considerable overlap among individuals in each of these categories, the percentages do not represent the same set of individuals. For example, many individuals who contribute financially are not involved in the campaign in any other way. Over half of the members of political clubs and organizations are not currently involved in any campaign activity, as minor studies have found earlier.[1] *Counting all forms of campaign activity well over 10 percent of the electorate are involved in some way.*

TABLE 5.1
Campaign Activities in 1952, 1956, 1960, 1964, and 1968

	1952	1956	1960	1964	1968
Do you belong to any political club or organization?	2%	3%	3%	4%	3%
Did you give any money or buy tickets or anything to help the campaign for one of the parties or candidates?	4%	10%	11%	11%	12%
Did you go to any political meetings, rallies, dinners, or things like that?	7%	7%	8%	8%	14%
Did you do any other work for one of the parties or candidates?	3%	3%	5%	5%	5%

Source: Survey Research Center, University of Michigan.

The increase of campaign activity has been greater among Republicans than Democrats or independents during this twelve-year period. By 1964 a large proportion of strongly partisan Republicans were giving money (about one-third) and attending meetings or rallies (about one-quarter), while among Democrats, independents, and less partisan Republicans less than one-tenth were active in these ways. In part these distributions are a result of

[1] See, for example, Robert Salisbury, "The Urban Party Organization Member," *Public Opinion Quarterly*, Vol. 29 (Winter, 1965-66), 553.

the higher socioeconomic position of Republicans; campaign contributions, for example, come disproportionately from the well-to-do. Higher income individuals not only can better afford to give, they are also easier to locate for solicitation. Although strong Republicans were fewer in number, they were more likely to engage in campaign activities in support of their party. The Republican Party advantage in campaign activity shows up most clearly in fund raising. The party, which includes a majority of the most wealthy in our society, contacts many more people than the Democrats for fund raising and receives contributions from many more. The result is that nationally the Republican Party raises more money through campaign solicitation than does the Democratic Party.

On the other hand, Democrats have about as many campaign actives as the Republicans, since there are so many more Democrats from which actives can be drawn. The Republicans still have more contributors, meeting-goers, and campaign workers, but the differences are not great. Table 5.2 shows how campaign workers in different partisanship categories were distributed in their preference for President in 1968. For whom or to what purpose these individuals campaigned is not known, but it is likely that almost all worked for the same party as their Presidential

TABLE 5.2
The Active Campaign Workers of 1968 according to Partisanship and Their Preference for President

	VOTED FOR			NON-VOTER WHO PREFERRED		
	Humphrey	Nixon	Wallace	Humphrey	Nixon	Wallace
Strong Democrat	23%			1	1	
Democrat	9	1				
Independent	5	12	1	1	4	
Republican		13			1	
Strong Republican		24			1	
Subtotal	37%	50%	1%	2%	7%	
Total				97%		
n =				75		

Source: Survey Research Center, University of Michigan.

vote. Nixon appears to have had more supporters actively involved in campaign work than did Humphrey. Wallace campaign workers were almost too rare to locate with a national sample. Although more campaign activity centers around Presidential candidates than other candidates, the Presidential race does not dominate the campaign to the exclusion of other races and general activity on behalf of the parties. In recent campaigns the relative advantage in numbers of workers enjoyed by the Republican Party does not appear to be overwhelming.

IMPACT OF POLITICAL CAMPAIGNS

A question that cannot be ignored is the impact of party activities and political campaigns generally on the American electorate. Although most professional politicians take for granted the efficacy of campaigns, scholarly analysis has often questioned their impact. For example, some campaigns to promote and publicize political ideas have had little impact. Furthermore, in most elections the overwhelming majority of voters decide how they will vote before the campaign begins. Beyond this the general low level of political information in the American electorate throws doubt on the ability of voters to absorb ideas during a campaign.

Perhaps two aspects of the problem should be distinguished in assessing the impact of political campaigns. First, there is the overall impact on the total electorate, but the evidence indicates that *most voters are not affected by political campaigns*. Second, there is the possibility that campaigning influences a small but crucial proportion of the electorate, and *many elections are close enough that the winning margin could be a result of the campaign*. It seems clear that professional politicians drive themselves and their organizations to influence every remaining undecided voter in the hope and expectation that they are providing or maintaining a winning margin.

One way of approaching the problem of campaign impact is to see how many voters make up their minds before the campaign starts. Table 5.3 shows that in Presidential elections from 1948 to 1968 voters made their vote choice at about the same time for most elections, and in most years about one-third of the electorate

TABLE 5.3
Distribution of Time of Decision on Vote Choice for President in 1948, 1952, 1956, 1960, 1964, and 1968

	1948	1952	1956	1960	1964	1968
Decided						
Before conventions	37%	34%	57%	30%	40%	33%
During conventions	28	31	18	30	25	22
During campaign	25	31	21	36	33	38
Don't remember, NA	10	4	4	4	3	7
Total	100%	100%	100%	100%	101%	100%
n =	424	1251	1285	1445	1126	1039

Source: Survey Research Center, University of Michigan.

decided before the conventions, another one-third decided during the conventions, and a final one-third decided during the campaign. In 1956 the rematch between Stevenson and an extremely popular Eisenhower was the most deviant election, where well over half of the voters made a decision on how they would vote before the convention. In 1960 and in 1968 exceptionally large numbers of voters reported making their vote choice during the campaign, and in 1968 7 percent of all voters recalled having made up their minds on election day.

Partisan differences between Democrats and Republicans are shown in Figure 5.1. In 1948, 1960, and 1968, the close elections during the period, the Democrats won the first two elections by coming from behind during the campaign period but Humphrey failed to do this. In 1948 and 1960, the Republicans had leads of 53 to 47 to 44 at the start of the campaigns, so Democrats overcame substantial leads in both elections. In 1952, 1956, and 1964 the eventual losers could not overcome leads of 60 to 40, 60 to 40, and 73 to 27. By the end of the conventions in 1956 and 1964, more voters had decided in favor of Eisenhower and Johnson, respectively, than their opponents would have by election day. In the extremely one-sided elections the winner's advantage accrues early, and during their respective campaigns Eisenhower and Johnson did not win substantially more additional voters to their side than their opponents. In 1968 the election was close at every stage of the campaign.

FIGURE 5.1

Distribution of Democratic and Republican Votes for President according to Time of Decision for 1948-1968

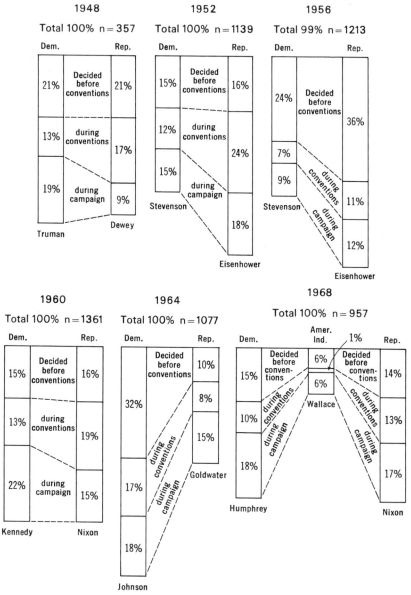

Source: Survey Research Center, University of Michigan.

aThese percentages were adjusted to make the survey data conform to the election results.

There are also differences in the decision times of partisans and independents because the loyal party votes line up early behind the party's candidate. In all recent elections the independents and weak partisans were more likely to make up their minds during the campaign, while the strong partisans characteristically make their decisions by the end of the conventions. To put it differently, the less committed are still undecided at the start of the campaign. *In fairly close elections this relatively uncommitted group can still swing the election either way, but in one-sided contests those who are still undecided during the campaign are too few in number to change the outcome.*

It is widely reported that the most interested voters make their vote decisions early and that the least interested voters remain undecided during the campaign. A great deal has been made of this generalization and its implications for campaign strategy. Essentially the consideration has taken this form: the least interested (and least concerned and least informed) are the only voters still available during the campaign; and, in order to influence them, very simple campaign appeals are necessary. The interested voters (mainly partisan and already committed) are held in line with appeals to party loyalty. This description is appropriate for some recent campaigns, but it is not necessarily a permanent characteristic of the American electorate. In fact the above description fits only the Eisenhower elections and perhaps the later Roosevelt elections. In 1960 there was a slight tendency for the least interested voters to decide early rather than late, and in 1964 and 1968 there was no difference in the time of decision of the most interested and least interested. In other words, under some circumstances interested voters are as likely as uninterested voters to enter the campaign still undecided on their vote choice. This is not to say that these interested voters are completely without preferences or that they are extremely well-informed. They are neither. But *it is not true that in all political campaigns the only voters still undecided at the start of the campaign are uninterested in politics.*

IMPACT OF PARTY CONTACT

One of the most direct attempts to influence voters is through door-to-door solicitation and telephoning. The reported impact of these efforts by party workers through personal contact is not impressive. Almost all voters report that they have not been influenced in their vote choice by party contacts. However, party contact may influence turnout and the level of financial contributions to the party. Since 1952 there has been a steady increase in the proportion of the electorate reporting that they have been contacted personally by one or both parties—from 11 percent in 1952 to 17 percent in 1956 to 20 percent in 1960 to 26 percent in 1964. The increase—about fifteen million more voters contacted in 1964 than in 1952—represents an enormous effort by party organizations. Whether it has much impact or not, personal contact is an activity which political organizations without great wealth can deliver, and since there is some evidence of payoff, it is an activity not likely to be abandoned. This evidence consists of findings which show that the party vote is somewhat greater than expected in areas of exceptional efforts in contacting voters.

MASS MEDIA AND POLITICAL CAMPAIGNS

At least as important as personal party contact during a political campaign is the contact made by candidates and party leaders through the mass media, mainly newspaper, radio, and television. Political information is transmitted by the mass media in two ways: through news stories and through advertising. There is no basis for assessing the relative impact of news versus advertising by the various media in political campaigns. Actually political scientists have seldom studied the impact of the content of the mass media, and in part this neglect is a reflection of the belief that campaigns are unimportant, that elections are decided before the campaign starts. Beyond this there is the belief that American voters receive little political information from the mass media or from any other source.

Several familiar patterns of attention are paid to the mass media. Individuals most interested in, and concerned about, politics pay greatest attention to politics in the mass media. Beyond this the better educated and the higher socioeconomic groups pay greater attention to the mass media as a source of political information. Also there is a tendency for strong partisans to pay more attention to the mass media than do other members of the electorate.

In social science by far the most important generalization about media attention has to do with "selective perception." Selective perception refers to a tendency to select information that conforms to one's ideas and values. Individuals allegedly avoid media content that would conflict with their present point of view and seek out information that reinforces their views. In the terms used in chapter 4 an individual selectively perceives mass media content in order to avoid or reduce dissonance. It is persuasive to argue that Democrats are more likely than Republicans to read news stories about Democratic candidates or to watch a Democratic television commercial. Common sense—if not empirical evidence—suggests that something like this does occur. However, there is no factual basis for believing that most voters successfully avoid political information that is in conflict with their present views. Most Americans are unavoidably exposed to political ideas and values with which they do not agree.

A clear example of a case in which selective perception almost certainly did not operate is the 1960 television debates between Kennedy and Nixon, when it would have been practically impossible to ignore one candidate and pay attention to the other. The debates illustrate the substantial impact that can come through the mass media under the right circumstances. Nearly everyone in the American electorate watched one or more television debates; and, according to several different public polls, about half of the voters reported that they were influenced by the debates in their evaluation of the candidates. Several millions of voters reported that they based their choice of candidates solely on the debates. Among voters reporting that the debates determined their vote choice, Kennedy held an advantage of three to one over Nixon.

No other opportunity in recent campaigns for winning so many uncommitted voters or winning over voters inclined to one's opponent has compared with the television debates of 1960. However, another significant political opportunity is the party nominating convention every four years. An increasingly large television audience is available to each party during the convention, but it appears difficult to hold the attention of the audience for extended periods of time, particularly if there is no contest for the Presidential nomination. Furthermore, the strong partisans follow their party's convention more intently than other members of the electorate. The 1968 Democratic convention in Chicago may represent an unprecedented failure to use this opportunity to the benefit of the nominee.

In 1964, for the first time in recent Presidential elections, books and political pamphlets were prominent. Many millions of volumes were sold or given away during the campaign, mainly by supporters of Barry Goldwater. We have no indication of the impact of this material and no way as yet of assessing the immediate and long-run influence of these materials.

The impact of mass media exposure on voting behavior in recent elections has been studied by Philip Converse of the Survey Research Center, who draws several conclusions based on the findings like those represented in Figure 5.2.[2] The most stable voters (whether stability is measured as during a campaign or between elections) are those who are highly attentive to mass media and those who pay no attention to media communication. *The shifting, unstable voters are more likely to be exposed moderately to mass media.* To restate this pattern: the least involved voters who receive no information from the mass media remain stable in their vote choice because no new information is introduced to change their vote. Their apathy and their lack of information protect them from forces which would alter their political preferences. The most involved voters who expose themselves to mass media and pay considerable attention to politics are sufficiently well-informed and secure in their vote choice so that some new information does not alter their commitment. The shifting voters are moderately involved in politics and moderately exposed to mass media, but seemingly new information can have a substantial impact on their vote choice since their commitment is less intense. To be sure, the less involved and less attentive an individual is, the less likely he is to bother to vote at all, so the above relationship applies only to those who do happen to vote. In non-Presidential elections several differences can be anticipated. Large numbers of citizens are exposed to no mass media, and there are much larger numbers of non-voters. At the other end of the curve there are fewer people with high media attention since so much less mass media content

[2] Philip Converse, "Information Flow and the Stability of Partisan Attitudes," *Public Opinion Quarterly,* Vol. 26 (Winter, 1962), 578-99.

FIGURE 5.2

The Hypothetical Relationship between Mass Media Attention and Stability of Voting Behavior

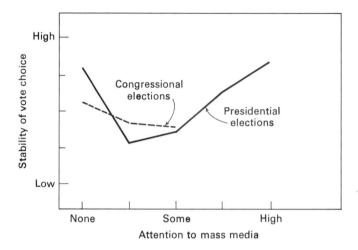

is devoted to non-Presidential campaigns. In effect, in "low salience" elections there are two types of media exposure, some and none; voting instability is about the same in both categories.

Still another aspect of the communication of political information is face-to-face discussion of ideas and values in the general public. Not much is known about the communication of political ideas through casual discussions with friends, family members, and fellow workers, but there is a widespread belief among social scientists that face-to-face communication accounts for much of the learning and reinforcing of political views in our society. Supposedly political ideas and information are transmitted in what is often called a "two-step flow of communication" from opinion elites (leaders in the society like politicians, businessmen, news commentators) to a minority of the public, opinion leaders, who in turn transmit the ideas to the remainder of the public.

CANDIDATE IMAGE AND POLITICAL CAMPAIGNS

Variable, short-run influences on voting choice do not appear to determine as many votes as do stable influences like partisanship.

On the other hand, these short-run influences cause the deviations from the basic party division. This deviation may determine the outcome of an election. One measure of short-run influences is the response to candidates during recent campaigns. As Table 5.4 shows, in 1952 and 1956 Eisenhower was much more favorably perceived by the electorate than was Stevenson; this advantage is one explanation for Eisenhower's victory in an electorate with more Democrats than Republicans. In 1964 not only did Johnson have the usual Democratic advantage in basic strength but he was also much more favorably viewed by the voters than was Goldwater. Goldwater was the only candidate in the four recent Presidential elections to be viewed more negatively than positively by the electorate. The 1960 election shows the short-run candidate image favoring Nixon over Kennedy rather strongly, but this was not enough for the Republican candidate to overcome the basic Democratic advantage.

The specific content of the candidates' image having varied greatly, no single pattern appears associated with either party. For example, a large proportion of the favorable and unfavorable references to Eisenhower in 1952 had to do with his experience as a military man; but by 1956 he was perceived almost entirely in other terms, mainly personal qualities rather than experience or qualifications. In 1964 the only strong point in Goldwater's image was "integrity," whereas many unfavorable references were made to his personal characteristics like "impulsiveness" and "trigger happy" and to his stands on issues. In 1960 Nixon's advantage over Kennedy rested mainly on a more favorable public impression of his qualifications and experience and an unfavorable reaction by many to Kennedy's Catholicism.

The perceptions of the parties contribute to the strength or weakness of candidates; but, as these perceptions may be quite changeable, they do not represent stable advantages or disadvantages for a party. Table 5.5 shows the changing perception of the parties in keeping the country out of war and emphasizes the loss and regaining by Republican Presidential candidates of their greatest asset in contests with Democrats. The loss of confidence in the Democrats had occurred by the elections of 1966 and was not connected with the events of 1968. Nixon's success in ending the war in Vietnam will probably determine the distribution of this attitude in the next few years.

TABLE 5.4
Total Number of References to Characteristics of Republican and Democratic Presidential Candidates, 1952-1964[a] (Survey Research Center, University of Michigan)

REFERENCES	1952		1956		1960		1964	
	Eisen-hower	Steven-son	Eisen-hower	Steven-son	Nixon	Ken-nedy	Gold-water	John-son
Positive	3153	2154	3485	1703	2790	2678	1505	3271
Negative	1415	1243	1378	1567	1214	1836	2815	1463
n =		1798		1791		1807		1570

Source: Angus Campbell, "Interpreting the Presidential Victory" in M. Cummings, ed., *The National Election of 1964* (Washington: Brookings Institution, 1966), p. 259, Table 8.1.

[a]The data in this table have been adjusted to remove the effect of differences in the number of respondents in the four surveys. The 1960 sample was taken as the base.

TABLE 5.5

Perceptions as to the Party Most Likely to Keep the United States out of War in the Ensuing Four Years

	1956	1960	1964	1968
Democrats would handle better	7%	15%	38%	13%
No party difference	45	46	46	49
Republicans would handle better	40	39	12	24
Don't know, not ascertained	8	10	4	14
Total	100%	100%	100%	100%

Source: P. Converse, A. Clausen, and W. Miller, "Electoral Myth and Reality," in E. Dreyer and W. Rosenbaum, eds., *Political Opinion and Electoral Behavior* (Belmont, Calif.: Wadsworth Publishing Co., 1966), p. 28, Table I, and Survey Research Center, University of Michigan.

Several characteristics of electoral behavior conflict with this description of the role of issues in influencing vote choice. For one thing, in most elections many voters are unaware of the stands taken by candidates on issues. It is common to find that voters believe the candidates they support agree with them on issues, and so voters may project their issue positions onto their favorite candidate more often than they decide to vote for a candidate on the basis of his position on issues. Furthermore, when voters agree on issues with the candidate they support, they may have adopted this position merely in order to agree with their candidate. Actually candidates and other political leaders frequently perform this function for members of the electorate; *they provide issue leadership for their following.* At the same time the candidates, after all, must campaign on the issues more or less; *the only determinants of vote choice which the candidates can manipulate during the campaign are the issue stands they take and the relative emphasis given the issues.*

There are limits to the issue influence. To appreciate this role of issues, their importance to individual voters must be considered. Table 5.6 displays the possibilities. Situation I is relatively uncommon in American elections, an election in which an issue (or issues) so dominates the electorate that issue stands by candidates determine the outcome. What is more likely, however, is that small collections of voters will care intensely about different issues and that some of these may, indeed, support

TABLE 5.6
Categories of Response to Issues and Candidates and Their Impact on the Electorate

Individual A's concern for Issue X initially	Individual A's view of candidate B's stand on Issue X	Candidate B's influence over Individual A on Issue X	Impact of Issue X on electorate
I. Issue X of great importance to Individual A	Individual A cares so much that he will find out how Candidate B stands on Issue X.	Candidate B has little influence over Individual A, and he will not be able to conceal his position on Issue X.	Individuals will oppose or support a candidate because of his stand on Issue X. If all individuals are deeply concerned with Issue X, it will have a great impact on voting.
II. Issue X of some interest to Individual A	Individual A may misperceive Candidate B's stand on Issue X, or he may be informed of his stand.	Candidate B may change Individual A's position on Issue X, or he may lead Individual A to think Issue X is more significant.	Issue X will not influence voting because individuals will learn their stand from a candidate they already support or support a candidate with a stand contrary to their own.
III. Issue X of no importance to Individual A	Individual A will neither know nor care about Candidate B's stand on Issue X.	Candidate B will not be able to influence Individual A or get Individual A to pay attention to Issue X.	Issue X will not influence turnout or votes for candidates. Even if the candidates treat Issue X as significant, it will not be consequential.

whichever candidate is closest to their position. In almost all elections a very small minority of voters is expected to vote on the basis of any single issue. Exceptional issues may create situations in which an election can be won with a single issue. The classic issue of American politics for achieving this has been the cluster of issues associated with the legacy of the Civil War, sometimes called the "bloody shirt." Currently the many matters associated with the "race issue" have this impact on large numbers of voters in some constituencies. Candidates for public office are usually searching for issues of this type which will help them. It is this constant search for such issues by the politically ambitious which leads to the assertion that in a democracy intense interests in the electorate cannot be long ignored.

Situation III, complete indifference to some issue, is quite common among the enormous range of topics that might be considered issues at any given time. A great many issues that are important to political leaders remain in this category for the general public. It has been particularly frustrating for American political leaders since World War II that the public has taken so little interest in foreign affairs. In general, American voters are assumed to care about domestic economic issues, if they care about any issue, and to be indifferent to foreign policy issues. A related but different emphasis casts this relationship in a broader pattern: *voters care intensely about an issue when they are suffering or perceive a threat;* usually the easiest threat to understand is economic; while the most difficult to comprehend are in the areas of foreign policy. Situation II falls somewhere in between the two extremes and applies to the few, major issues of an ordinary campaign. The individual voters can be aroused to take a stand on the issue in support of their party or candidate and be made to care moderately about the issue. The voters recognize its importance but do not feel a great personal stake in the matter.

ISSUE CANDIDACY

For several decades election analysts have been free to ignore third parties or independent candidates and to concentrate on the Republican and Democratic Parties. But 1968 provided the first Presidential election in the era of public-opinion surveys in which a sizable proportion of the vote went to a candidate not on the tickets of the major parties, although earlier in the century three-man races occurred in 1912 and 1924. Moreover, every year in state and local elections, candidacies not associated with either major party are significant and often dominate elections. It is certainly not true that most elections in the United States are characterized by stable competition between a Democrat and a Republican.

Recent Presidential elections prior to 1968 have been atypical in several respects. For one thing, as they attract great attention in the mass media, they are the focus of great effort by both political parties. For these and other reasons Presidential elections attract an exceptionally large turnout by American standards; and, of course, the main competition has been limited to a race between a Republican and a Democrat. Thus, large numbers of voters who ordinarily did not participate in elections were involved in well-publicized and competitively fought races between the two major parties. In this setting we have consistently found that the most significant explanation of vote choice was partisanship and that the second most important factor was the personal characteristics of the candidates. Under those circumstances, the role of issues was masked by parties and candidates, but 1968 provided an opportunity, through examination, to assess the role that issues may play in Presidential vote choice. Wallace, who was practically without a party, represents an issue candidacy.

Actually, there is a constant barrage of new issues heralded by parties and candidates attempting to attract the public's attention and to develop a basis of successful electoral appeals. Presumably most efforts fail because the issues lack salience or occasionally because new candidates and parties fail to become identified with an issue. Ordinarily the major parties are expected to absorb the potential support associated with salient issues. However, *candidates outside the established parties can make successful appeals when they are identified with a salient issue position which is not reflected by the established parties.*

An examination of two issues of the 1968 campaign, Vietnam and school integration, which were introduced in chapter 4, shows the significance of issues for the Wallace vote. Among voters opposing school integration and favoring a stronger stand in Vietnam, Wallace received more than twice as many votes as his national average. Among voters favoring school integration and supporting an immediate withdrawal from Vietnam, only 1 percent supported Wallace. This pattern contrasts with Nixon voters, whose attitudes did not deviate particularly from the average distribution. Humphrey's support was disproportionately found among voters who favored school integration and immediate withdrawal from Vietnam.

Wallace obviously had a differential and substantial appeal which appears related to issues. Part of the analysis of the 1968 campaign has focused on Wallace's impact on the vote for Nixon and Humphrey. Table 5.7 shows that the Wallace vote was drawn strongly from Democratic Party identifiers, while at the same time Wallace voters were much more likely to prefer Nixon to Humphrey as a second choice. While it is not possible to say what would have actually happened without Wallace in the race, Table 5.7 suggests that Wallace cost Nixon many more votes than he did Humphrey. An even more surprising aspect of the Wallace vote was the disproportionate support which he drew from young people. It appears that older people with stronger and more long-standing party loyalties remained with the candidates of their traditional parties (or perhaps returned to them in the course of the campaign). Young people with their greater independence and more conservative issue positions were a stronger base of support for Wallace.

TABLE 5.7
Party Identification and Candidate Preference among Wallace Voters in 1968

	Democrats	Independents	Republicans
Prefer Humphrey to Nixon	13%	5	5
Prefer Humphrey and Nixon equally	17	1	1
Prefer Nixon to Humphrey	31	7	20
			100%
			n = 110

Source: Recomputed from Philip E. Converse, Warren E. Miller, Jerrold G. Rusk, and Arthur C. Wolfe, "Continuity and Change in American Politics: Parties and Issues in the 1968 Election," *American Political Science Review,* Vol. 63 (December, 1969), 1091, Table 3.

The campaign year of 1968 offered another issue candidacy with the efforts of Eugene McCarthy to capture the Democratic Party's nomination for the Presidency. Certainly an overriding feature of the McCarthy campaign was opposition to the war in Vietnam and a demand that the war be ended. Nevertheless, the salience of his stand was so low that in New Hampshire, where he made such a surprisingly strong showing, more of the voters who supported him did so for hawkish reasons than for doveish ones.[3]

The opportunities offered by issues in 1968 to candidates outside the established parties were mainly opportunities on the conservative side of the two parties. Contrary to the hopes often expressed by liberals, the big blocs of voters to be won away from the traditional parties by issue appeals were voters who favored segregation, supported escalating the war in Vietnam, and advocated tougher law enforcement. This is not a necessary or permanent condition, and, presumably, if one or both of the major parties shifts to win over these conservative voters, there will be larger numbers of liberal voters available to new appeals.

By way of summary, several hypotheses can be offered about issue candidacies. Issue candidates will attract support when their position is not reflected in established parties and when the issue is highly salient. Most issue candidacies probably fail because the issues involved are not salient for the electorate. Perhaps some such candidacies fail because the candidate does not become identified with the issue; but, if the issue is highly salient and ignored by others, identification with it should be assured.

Issue candidates should do best when mobilization by established parties is low, as in primaries, local elections, etc. In other words, traditional loyalties undermine new issue candidacies. Early in October in the campaign of 1968 Wallace showed a peak of strength which steadily declined as election day approached. Quite probably the traditional loyalties did not begin to exert their pull until the last month of the campaign, making it more and more difficult for Wallace to hold voters. In low turnout elections, enthusiasts—whether partisans or issue based—will be at maximum strength. Higher turnout brings voters who are less interested, less aware, and presumably more difficult to influence;

[3] Recomputed from Philip E. Converse, Warren E. Miller, Jerrold G. Rusk, and Arthur C. Wolfe, "Continuity and Change in American Politics: Parties and Issues in the 1968 Election," *American Political Science Review,* Vol. 63 (December, 1969), 1092.

but it also brings voters less committed to established parties and thus more susceptible to other appeals. Presumably issue candidacies, like ordinary party candidacies, rise or fall with their ability to appeal to a relatively uninterested group of voters.

A major aspect of the Survey Research Center analysis of national elections is the attempt developed by Donald Stokes[4] to measure attitudinal forces influencing Presidential vote choices. His "component analysis" shown for four Presidential elections in Figure 5.3 takes into account the net impact of an attitudinal component on the vote and the strength of association between the attitudes and vote choice. The six attitudinal components represented by the bars as having a net pro-Democratic or pro-Republican impact in Figure 5.3 show the short-run forces causing deviations from basic partisan alignments in the electorate. This component analysis dramatizes the disastrous impact of the Goldwater candidacy in 1964. The bars also indicate the usual Republican advantage on foreign policy issues and a slight tendency for domestic issues to benefit Democratic candidates. The Democrats consistently benefit from the widespread perception that Democrats are likely to help groups in the electorate with which voters identify. At the very least these attitudinal components represent the ideas and words which voters use to describe their feelings about the candidates.

During the conventions and the brief period of the campaign, political parties cannot do much about the basic partisan strength of each side; therefore they concentrate on presenting candidate images and issue positions calculated to have greatest appeal to the uncommitted voters. Even if the outcome of an election is not substantially affected by party strategies, the content of the campaign and the meaning the election comes to have for leaders and the public are created by these strategies. Figure 5.3 can be viewed as measures of the content of the campaign and the meaning it has for the voters.

TYPES OF ELECTIONS

The late V. O. Key, a major political analyst of American elections, devised a set of categories for classifying elections. While

[4] Angus Campbell et al., *The American Voter* (New York: John Wiley and Sons, 1960), pp. 524-31.

FIGURE 5.3
Attitudinal Component Analysis of the 1952, 1956, 1960, and 1964 Presidential Elections (Survey Research Center, University of Michigan)

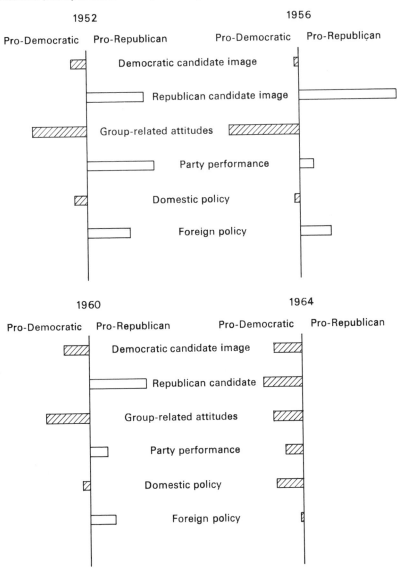

Source: These bar graphs were made from data provided in Donald Stokes, "Some Dynamic Elements of Contests for the Presidency," *American Political Science Review,* Vol. 60 (March, 1966), 19-28.

more elaborate versions of this scheme exist, these three categories will do for present purposes. The three types of elections are "maintaining," "deviating," and "realigning" elections.

A maintaining election is one in which the stable, underlying partisan division in the electorate is directly reflected in the vote. The short-run forces associated with candidates and issues are not sufficient to change the outcome from what would be expected on the basis of normal party strength. By this definition the 1948 election of Truman, the 1960 election of Kennedy, and the 1964 election of Johnson were maintaining elections with the basic Democratic advantage reflected in Democratic victories. The Eisenhower victories of 1952 and 1956 and the Nixon victory in 1968 were deviating elections in which the short-run forces were strong enough to overcome the underlying partisan alignment; the candidates and issues caused a deviation from the outcome expected on the basis of normal party strength. According to an analysis of expected vote for President compared with Congressional voting over the full history of the United States,[5] the only candidates to inspire an extra "bonus vote" were popular military heroes, although not all of these victories were deviating elections.

Realigning elections have been uncommon in American electoral history; the period of 1928 and 1932 provided the most recent illustration. In realigning elections there is a substantial shift in the underlying partisan division, such shifts presumably accompanying rather drastic social disruptions like those associated with severe depressions and wars. Realigning elections or realigning periods account for the basic shifts in electoral patterns, but most political change is associated with more temporary deviating patterns.

The break in patterns of party voting in the 1890s is so closely associated with a major economic depression that the shift is quite similar to the early 1930s. As in 1930 the major break came in the Congressional elections of 1894 two years before the Presidential election in which McKinley defeated Bryan. Though the election has been interpreted as a conservative victory in the North, this should not be exaggerated. The Democratic Party in

[5] Charles Sellers, "The Equilibrium Cycle in Two-party Politics," *Public Opinion Quarterly,* Vol. 29 (Spring, 1965), 22. The Presidents were Washington, Jackson, W. H. Harrison, Taylor, Grant, and Eisenhower.

power was under Cleveland's conservative leadership, and rightly or wrongly the Democrats were held responsible for the depression just as the Republicans were after 1929. The Congressional elections of 1894 broke patterns of political loyalty that had survived the Civil War in many areas. In one hundred years of electoral patterns the only dramatic shifts of basic partisan loyalty are directly related to major economic crises. While subsequent Presidential campaigns undoubtedly influenced these patterns, the major shifts did not appear to depend on the Presidential candidates of either 1896 or 1932. The main impetus appears to be a rejection of the party in power when the crisis occurs.

We cannot be certain that the shifts in basic partisan strength will be dramatic and that they result from social crises of some sort. It is also possible that shifts in party following will occur gradually. The slow erosion of party followers over a decade could be just as important as more rapid change for the electoral system. The general assumption has been that only major social crises have the impact necessary to alter partisan loyalties, but the fundamental point is that the individual must be under such pressure that he changes his party identification. For this to happen to large numbers of people quickly, a social crisis is probably necessary; but, for this to happen to a large number of people over a decade or so, independent events like individual social mobility might accomplish the same thing.

MEANING OF AN ELECTION

A persistent question in American politics is what election results mean. Politicians and news commentators spend much time and energy interpreting and explaining the outcome. It is easy to exaggerate the difficulties in assigning meaning to elections, but the most important element is usually quite clear—the winner. Elections are primarily a mechanism for selecting certain governmental leaders and, just as important, for removing leaders from office and preventing others from gaining office. Nevertheless, an effort is often made to discover the policy implications of patterns of voting and to read meaning into the outcome of elections. This effort raises two problems for analysis; first, the policy implications of winning and losing candidates' issue stands, and second, the issue content of the voters' decisions.

It is perfectly appropriate to attribute policy significance to an election on the basis of the policy preferences of the winning candidates so long as it is not implied that the voters had these policy implications in mind when they voted. That is, it is appropriate to observe that the election outcome means lower taxes or an expanded program because the victor has pledged to lower taxes or an expanded program. But it is very difficult to establish that the voters' preferences have certain policy meaning or that the votes for a particular candidate provide a policy mandate. There are several obstacles to stating simply what policies are implied by the voters' behavior. In many elections the voters are unaware of the candidates' stands on issues, and sometimes the voters are mistaken in their perceptions of candidates' stands. Even if every voter knew that candidate A supported issue position X and that candidate B opposed X, this alone would provide no basis for concluding that voters' preference for candidate A was based on his support of X.

Furthermore, many voters are not concerned with issues in a campaign but vote according to their party loyalty. Presumably their vote has no particular policy significance but reflects a general preference for one party over another. If only those voters for whom the issues have some relevance to their decision are considered, statements can be made about the issues which helped a candidate win.

But at this point there is another difficulty. A crucial minority may swing to candidate C and give him a narrow victory because of his support of issue Y, which is highly salient for this minority. It would be possible to say that candidate C won because of his support of issue Y, and yet it might also be true that the vast majority of voters who supported candidate C were opposed to issue Y but supported candidate C for other reasons. Is the election a mandate for or against policy Y? There is no correct answer to this question. What happens in the political system is that candidate C will try to select a course of action with respect to issue Y which will least jeopardize his chances for reelection. Candidate C has considerable freedom under these circumstances to interpret his victory with respect to issue Y. Most election outcomes are just this vague and conflicting with respect to most issues. This is a partial explanation of the failure of the American political system to impose policy stands on elected officials.

On the other hand, generally there is no intense, widespread opposition to the stands of the candidate among his supporters. Voters will often vote for candidates who hold views not shared by the voters, but these views are on matters of little interest to the voters. Presumably voters seldom support candidates who hold views with which they disagree intensely. In other words there is no intense, widespread opposition to the policies of the winning candidate, but there may or may not be support for his policies. The main explanation of electoral support is still partisanship.

Campaigns and conventions, media coverage, party activities, and general discussions provide the electorate with political information. For most the information is insufficient to motivate them to vote. For many voters, campaigns inspire some partisan enthusiasm and reinforce usual political commitments, and for others the campaign provides information which disturbs their customary vote patterns. The candidates and parties concentrate on arousing sympathetic responses in the electorate, but they must attempt this with an electorate whose opinions and loyalties are fairly set by the start of a campaign. For the most part they must work with situations they cannot greatly change. Campaign strategies aim at gaining an advantage in turnout among one's voters and at publicizing themes and symbols which arouse favorable sympathies. *The outcome of an election is mainly a result of the political preferences and patterns in the electorate and only slightly a result of the parties' strategy and maneuvering.* Since both parties in ordinary constituencies make substantial efforts during campaigns, their efforts may cancel one another. But neither party can afford to reduce its efforts. Furthermore, even a relatively modest impact can change the outcome of close elections.

American elections are hardly a classic model of democracy with rational, well-informed voters making dispassionate decisions. On the other hand, Americans provide an acceptable electoral opportunity for parties and candidates to attempt to win or hold public office. The electorate appears capable upon occasion to respond to issue appeals both positively and negatively but does not appear easily moved by most appeals. Traditional loyalties dominate electoral patterns and apparently reduce the possible instability of the electorate and its vulnerability to most appeals. In recent years the electorate has offered the parties modest

opportunities to gain votes without offering extreme temptations
to reckless appeals.

Survey Research Methods

So many of the data in this book have come from survey research and so much of the analysis reported has been based on findings from survey research that some description of these methods may be necessary to establish their appropriateness. During the last thirty years social scientists have developed an impressive array of techniques for discovering and measuring individual attitudes and behavior. Basically survey research relies on giving a standard questionnaire to the individuals to be studied; and in most major studies of the national electorate trained interviewers ask the questions and record the responses in a face-to-face interview with each respondent. A few studies depend on the respondents to fill out the questionnaires themselves without using interviewers.

There are four data collection phases of survey research: (1) sampling, (2) interviewing, (3) questionnaire constructing, and (4) coding. At most points the methods of the Survey Research Center at the University of Michigan will be described.

SAMPLING

It may seem inappropriate to analyze the entire American electorate with studies composed of fewer than two thousand individuals, which is about the number of respondents in the studies used in this book. It would be prohibitively expensive to interview the entire electorate, and the only way to study public opinion nationally is by interviewing relatively few individuals who accurately represent the entire electorate. *Probability sampling is the method used to assure that the individuals selected for interviewing will be representative of the total population.*

Probability sampling attempts to select respondents in such a way that every individual in the population has an equal chance of being selected for interviewing. If the respondents are selected in this way, the analyst can be confident that the characteristics of the sample are approximately the same as those of the whole population. It would be impossibly difficult to make a list of every adult in the United States and then draw names from the list randomly, so the Survey Research Center departs from such strict random procedures in three basic ways: the sample is *stratified, clustered,* and *of households.*

Since stratification means that random selection occurs within subpopulations, in the United States the sample is customarily selected within regions to guarantee that all sections are represented and within communities of different sizes as well. Clustering means that within the geographical areas selected for sampling the interviews are concentrated in order to reduce the costs and inconvenience for interviewers. Finally, the Survey Research Center samples households rather than individuals (although within households individuals are sampled and interviewed); this means that within sampling areas households are enumerated and selected at random. (This sampling procedure means that there are no interviews on military bases, in hospitals and prisons, or in other places where people do not live in households.)

An alternative procedure for selecting respondents is quota sampling and is employed commonly by commercial polling organizations. The areas where interviews are to be made may be picked by stratified sampling procedures, but at the last stage of selection the interviewer is given discretion to choose respondents according to quotas. Quotas usually cover several social characteristics, but the intention is to create a collection of respondents with proportions of quota-controlled characteristics identical to those in the population. For example, the quota might call for half the respondents to be men, half to be women; for one-third to be grade school educated, one-third high school educated, and one-third college educated; and so forth. The advantage of this procedure is that it is much faster and less expensive than probability sampling, but the disadvantages are severe. With quota sampling the analyst cannot have confidence that respondents are representative of the total population because the interviewers introduce conscious or unconscious biases when selecting respondents. Both methods of sampling depend heavily on the ability and integrity of the interviewers, but probability sampling does not permit interviewers to introduce biases. Most statistical manipulations depend on using probability sampling.

INTERVIEWING

The selection of the sample depends on the interviewer, but even more important is the role of the interviewer in asking questions of the respondent and in recording the answers. Motivated, well-trained interviewers are crucial to the success of survey research. The interviewer has several major responsibilities: first, he selects the respondent according to sampling instructions; second, the interviewer must develop rapport with the respondent so that he will be willing to go through with the interview, which may last an hour or more; third, the interviewer must ask the questions in a friendly way and encourage the respondent to answer fully without distorting the answers; finally, the interviewer must record the answers of the respondent fully and accurately. In order to accomplish these tasks with a high level of proficiency the survey organizations train and retrain a permanent staff of interviewers.

QUESTIONNAIRE CONSTRUCTING

Ordinarily in survey questionnaires several types of questions will be used. Public opinion surveys began years ago with forced choice questions to which a respondent was asked to give a simple answer. For example, forced choice questions frequently take the form of stating a position on public policy and asking the respondent to "agree" or "disagree" with the statement. The analysis in chapter 4 was based on forced choice questions on public policy used in Survey Research Center questionnaires in which respondents were asked to "agree strongly," "agree," "disagree," or "disagree strongly." Some respondents give qualified answers that do not fit into these prearranged categories, or have no opinions.

The major innovation associated with the Survey Research Center is an alternative form of questioning called "open-ended." Open-ended questions give the respondent the opportunity to express his opinion in his own way without being forced to select among categories provided by the questionnaire. Questions like "Is there anything in particular you like about the Democratic Party?" or "What are the most important problems facing the country today?" permit the respondent to answer in his own terms. Survey Research Center interviewers encourage respondents to answer such questions as fully as they can with "probes" like "Could you tell me more about that?" "Anything else?" and similar queries that draw forth more discussion. There is no doubt that open-ended questions are a superior method of eliciting accurate expressions of opinion.

There are two major disadvantages in open-ended questioning: one is that it places much more of a burden on interviewers to record the responses, and the other is that the burden of reducing the many responses to a dimension that can be analyzed is left for the coders. For example, in the United States if people are asked, "Do you think of yourself as a Democrat, a Republican or an independent?" almost all of the responses will fit usefully into the designated categories:

1. Democrat
2. Independent
3. Republican
4. Other party
5. I'm nothing, apolitical
6. Don't know
7. Refused to say
8. Not ascertained

On the other hand, if a relatively unstructured, open-ended question is used, like "How do you think of yourself politically?" some people would answer with "Democrat," "Republican," etc., but many others would give answers that were quite different and not easily compared with the partisan categories. Often analysts intend to force responses into a single dimension like partisanship whether the respondents would have volunteered an answer along that dimension or not. This is essential if they are to develop single dimensions for analytic purposes. Modern survey research includes questions and techniques considerably more complex than these examples for establishing dimensions, but for the most part these methods have not been applied in political studies.

CODING

Once the interviewers administer the questionnaires to respondents, the coders take over and reduce the verbal information to a numerical form according to a "code." The numeric information, unlike verbal information, can be processed and manipulated by high-speed data processing equipment. The coders' task may be simple or complex. For example, to code the respondent's sex requires a simple code:

1. Male
2. Female

This means that on an IBM card which contains information on the respondent a column will be designated for indicating the respondent's sex. A "1" punch in the column will indicate men and a "2" punch will indicate women. The code shown above for partisan categories gives the numbers that would stand for various responses.

Some coding is very complicated in that it requires elaborate arrays of categories and many columns on an IBM card. For example, coding of the responses to a question like "Is there anything in particular you don't like about the Democratic Party?" might include fifty or a hundred categories and these categories would cover such details as: "I like the party's farm policies," "I like the party's tax program," "I've just always been a Democrat." Some codes require the coders to make judgments about the respondents' answers, and in political surveys these codes have covered judgments on the level of sophistication of the respondents' answers and judgments as to the main reason for respondents' vote choices. After the coders have converted the verbal information into numbers according to the coding instructions, the numbers are punched into IBM cards and readied for analysis. At this point the survey research process ends; the political analyst takes over to make what use of the data he can.

There are a number of good texts on survey research methods. The Survey Research Center has a *Manual for Interviewers* and a *Manual for Coders;*[1] these provide simple, thorough introductions to two phases of the data collection process. Leslie Kish's *Survey Sampling*[2] is by far the most authoritative and difficult work on sampling. Kahn and Cannel have provided a description and defense of the Survey Research Center interviewing in *The Dynamics of Interviewing.*[3] The best discussion of the use of survey research from the perspective of the social analyst is Herbert Hyman's *Survey Design and Analysis.*[4] The general introductions to social science methods include discussions of survey research; the best are Festinger and Katz, *Research Methods in the Behavioral Sciences,*[5] and Selltiz et al., *Research Methods in Social Relations.*[6] All major survey research organizations can provide descriptions of their methods, but the best single collection of questionnaires, codes, and other methods from major political studies is available through the Inter-university Consortium for Political Research located at the University of Michigan.

[1] These manuals are available from the Survey Research Center at the University of Michigan.

[2] Leslie Kish, *Survey Sampling* (New York: John Wiley and Sons, 1965).

[3] Robert Kahn and Charles Cannel, *The Dynamics of Interviewing* (New York: John Wiley and Sons, 1957).

[4] Herbert Hyman, *Survey Design and Analysis* (Glencoe: The Free Press, 1955).

[5] Leon Festinger and Daniel Katz, eds., *Research Methods in the Behavioral Sciences* (New York: The Dryden Press, 1953).

[6] Claire Selltiz et al., *Research Methods in Social Relations* (New York: Holt, Rinehart and Winston, 1959).